A Fresh Look at Grading and Reporting in High Schools

A Fresh Look at Grading and Reporting in High Schools

Sandra Herbst
Anne Davies, Ph. D.

connect2learning

© 2014 Text, Sandra Herbst, A. Davies Duncan Holdings Inc.
© 2014 Book Design, Building Connections Publishing, Inc.

All rights reserved. Except as noted, no part of this book may be reproduced or utilized in any form or by any means, electronic or mechanical, including photocopying, recording, or by any information storage and retrieval system, without permission in writing from the publisher.

Printed and bound in Canada by Hignell Book Printing.

16 15 14   5 4 3 2

Book Design: START Communications
Cover Art and Design: Anne Davies
Project Management: Judith Hall-Patch

Library and Archives Canada Cataloguing in Publication

Davies, Anne, 1955-
    A fresh look at grading and reporting in high schools / Anne Davies and Sandra Herbst.

Includes bibliographical references.
ISBN 978-0-9867851-6-0

    1. Grading and marking (Students)--Canada. 2. Education, Secondary--Canada. I. Herbst, Sandra, 1970- II. Title.

LB3054.C3D39 2013   373.127'20971   C2013-901222-2

Additional copies of this book may be purchased from:

connect2learning

2449D Rosewall Crescent
Courtenay, BC V9N 8R9
CANADA
1-800-603-9888 (North America only)
1-250-703-2920
1-250-703-2921 (Fax)
books@connect2learning.com
www.connect2learning.com

Discounts available on bulk orders.

Contents

Foreword ix
Introduction xiii

Chapter 1 Preparing for Quality Classroom Assessment 1
Chapter 2 Activating and Engaging Learners Through Quality Assessment 27
Chapter 3 After the Learning: Evaluating and Reporting to Others 53

Afterword: Until the Next Time 69
References 71
Appendix A: Pushing Back: What About These Challenges? 77
Appendix B: Four-Quadrant Planning Questions 89

Dedicated to the young people in our lives:
Kara and Colin
Kayla and Dakota

Foreword

"It is also important that summative assessment procedures are in harmony with the procedures of formative assessment and that they are transparent, with judgments supported by evidence so that all involved can have trust in the results."
Assessment Reform Group (2006, p.1)

It is no wonder that educators, parents, and students are experiencing such significant cognitive dissonance surrounding evaluation and reporting. Informed standards-based grading and reporting today is different from the grading and reporting that educators used during the twentieth century, whether the issue is about assigning zeros, what counts as reliable and valid evidence, or how teachers can get it all done and done well while still having a life.

Successfully responding to the challenging task of informed reporting today is possible only when methods unique to classroom assessment are properly implemented. Done well, classroom evaluation and reporting:

- reflect a student's most consistent and more recent pattern of performance in relation to agreed-upon standards, criteria, and pre-determined levels of quality
- occur after students have been involved in understanding quality by co-constructing criteria and *after* students have had the time and opportunity to learn
- are given in relation to the full range of educational standards or outcomes and are based upon a wide array of evidence of learning selected because of its alignment with outcomes and standards
- are understood by students (both expectations and acceptable evidence) and are derived from evidence present, not absent (thus devoid of practices such as grading on a curve, averaging)
- do not reflect data related to factors such as effort, attitude, attendance, and punctuality, as the effect of those factors is evident in the quality and amount of the evidence of learning

- reflect informed teacher professional judgment of the level of quality of student work in relation to the criteria of success given the standards and outcomes
- take place in an environment where there are quality-assurance and control processes that are validated and anchored in collaborative conversation and analysis of student work against agreed-upon criteria – by teachers, and across grade levels and subjects – in order to ensure consistency and fairness in judgment

Effective classroom assessment supports learning and leads to standards-based reporting that respects the structure of each unique subject area or discipline, supports student learning and achievement, communicates effectively with a range of audiences, and fulfills our required legal and regulatory responsibilities. There is no single right answer but rather many right answers that reflect the discipline being taught and the ways of learning and knowing that students need to demonstrate.

Step-by-step, this book describes how you can effectively work through complexity to something much, much better–that is, a powerful, practical, and informed standards-based grading and reporting process. We are expressing complex ideas in a set of easy-to-do steps, using straightforward language. However, do not be deceived by the simplicity of the ideas we share. Alfred North Whitehead once wrote, "...the only simplicity to be trusted is the simplicity to be found on the far side of complexity." We have found that it is only when we truly understand the complexity of grading and reporting that we can begin to take practical next steps towards positive change. This fresh look at grading and reporting arises from the important work of transforming classroom assessment.

Throughout the text, in shaded boxes, we have provided responses to some common questions that people ask us. Some might view these as "yah buts" or "push backs." But we view them as opportunities to engage in dialogue – to seek to understand the viewpoints of others before we ourselves reach full understanding. We identify each one as a *What About . . . ?* These *What About . . . ?* shaded boxes throughout the text are short. See Appendix A on page 77 for more information about each one.

> **What About...?**
>
> *Assessment isn't about helping my students learn. It is something that comes at the end of learning.*
>
> Involving students throughout the learning process, including involving them in their own assessment, helps students understand what they are learning. Being able to look at their work and compare it to samples or criteria provides them with specific information about what they might need in order to keep doing it and what they might need to do differently.
>
> *(To read more about this, see What About F-1? on page 77.)*

This book results from our work over many years working alongside secondary teachers, as well as school and system leaders. We have not attached specific teacher, school, or district names, as our ideas developed from the rich conversations that took place among educators across time and physical location and because today's proven practices and solutions, given today's rules, regulations, and technology options, may not be those of tomorrow; we do not wish to limit future learning and change. Proven practices do not stand still; rather, they evolve when teachers, schools, and systems seek to respond positively to the complexity of the times.

We thank all the educators who have helped us take away anything unnecessary that might lie between a teacher and a successful classroom assessment plan.

We trust that these student-, teacher-, administrator-, and parent-tested ideas help you find your way to grading and reporting processes that are both possible and practical in your context, so that your actions support student learning and help you to have a life beyond the classroom – not just during report card time, but all year long.

Introduction

"Begin with the End in Mind means to begin each day, task, or project with a clear vision of your desired direction and destination, and then continue by flexing your proactive muscles to make things happen."

Stephen Covey

The essential components of *A Fresh Look at Grading and Reporting in High Schools* both model and mirror effective practice: preparing for learning, teaching, and assessment; engaging students in assessment in support of their learning; and reporting the learning to others.

Preparing to teach, and therefore, preparing for student learning is critical. Within an instructional framework, it identifies what comes *before*. For our purposes, we organize the *before* around the following four professional and instructional responsibilities when we:

- determine the learning destination
- research the expected quality levels
- plan to collect reliable and valid evidence of learning
- collect baseline evidence of learning

What happens *during* the learning calls us to constantly adjust, revise, and refine. As we activate and engage our learners, we ensure that we:

- describe the learning destination and expected quality
- involve students and provide time and support for them to learn
- teach to student needs based on assessment evidence
- collect reliable and valid evidence of learning

Then, *at the end of learning*, we evaluate the degree to which learning has occurred and report that to others. This requires that we:

- finalize the collection of evidence of learning
- make informed professional judgments
- report learning and achievement using required format
- involve students in the reporting process

This instructional framework – which includes before, during, and after – is both familiar and powerful, and it is a proven practice in achieving informed classroom assessment, evaluation, and reporting.

Let's begin building your own classroom assessment plan by defining important terms relating to classroom assessment. Note that the terms *assessment* and *evaluation* need to be carefully used because they mean different things. Assessment occurs when teachers observe and coach students as they practice and learn. Assessment, at the classroom level, is sometimes referred to as *formative assessment*, particularly when the information that arises is used to inform instruction. Evaluation is the "show time"; it happens at the end of the practice. Assessment occurs *during* the learning, while evaluation occurs at the end of the learning.

This terminology makes sense if you consider the etymology of the words in English. The root of *assessment* is the word *assess*, which means "to sit beside." The root of the word *evaluation* is *value*, which means "to judge." So, when we assess, "...we are gathering information about student learning that informs our teaching and helps students learn more....When we evaluate, we decide whether or not students have learned what they needed to learn and how well they have learned it. Evaluation is a process of reviewing the evidence and determining its value" (Davies, 2011, p. 1). It is especially important to understand that when classroom-based assessment is done well, it leads to further learning. When classroom-based evaluation is done well, it leads to clarity of communication about learning and achievement and grading decisions that are accurate reflections of learning.

The Assessment Reform Group (2002) and Stiggins (2002) coined two additional terms that have supported a deeper understanding of classroom assessment: *Assessment for Learning* and *Assessment of Learning*. Assessment *for* learning is formative assessment, plus the deep involvement of learners in the assessment process. Assessment *of* learning is the same as summative assessment, or evaluation. When assessment *for* learning is done well, teachers have the information they need to teach to emerging needs so all students are learning *and* students have the information they need to self-regulate and self-monitor their way to success. When assessment *of* learning is done well, teachers' informed professional judgment is more reliable and more valid than external tests (ARG, 2006; Burger et al., 2009). (See Figure I-2 on page xviii for the difference between large-scale and classroom assessment.)

Classroom assessment supports student learning and then, when the learning time is over, evaluates what individuals know, can do, and can articulate. To illustrate, let's consider three different assessment, evaluation, and reporting examples: a parachute course, an employment selection process, and a band concert. As you read, notice what is similar and what is different among these examples.

1. A Parachute Course

In *Making Classroom Assessment Work* (2011), Davies uses an illustration first shared by Michael Burger (see Figure I-1). Consider this: Three students are taking a course on how to pack a parachute. Imagine that the class average is represented by a solid line. Student A initially scored very high, but his scores have dropped as the end of the course approaches. Student B's evaluations are erratic. Sometimes he does very well and sometimes he doesn't. The teacher has a hard time predicting from day to day how he will do. Student C did very poorly in relation to the others in class for the first two-thirds of the course but has finally figured out how to successfully pack a parachute. Which of these students would you want to pack your parachute? Student A? Student B? Student C? Most people would choose Student C because they want the chute to open successfully; after all, a parachute course is standards-based or outcomes-based. The problem is that traditional thinking about grades and evidence of learning was in effect, so all numerical data was valued equally with no professional judgment being made about which numerical data should be included and why. So, in the past, Student C did not pass the course. When his marks were tallied and averaged, they weren't high enough. Student A and Student B did pass.

Figure I-1 ▼

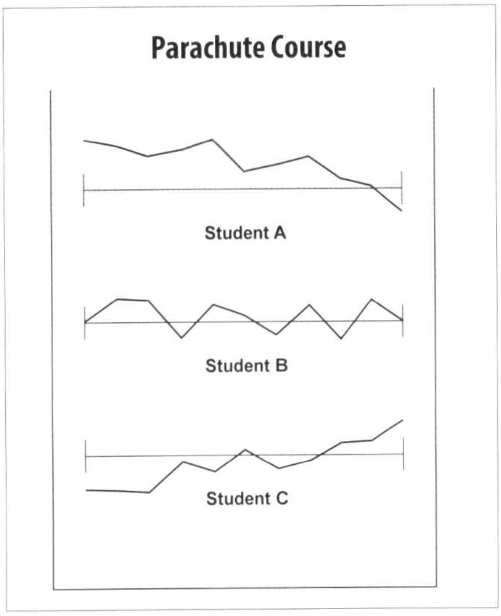

From Davies, *Making Classroom Assessment Work*, 3rd Edition, 2. Used with permission.

2. An Employment Selection Process

Consider the job selection process for a teaching position. At the end of the process, a person or a panel of people determined whether you were suitable for the position. Were you valued as the best candidate? What you did up to that point is the foundation of the final decision. Were your references positive, based on others' interactions and experiences with you? Were your student teaching blocks or term positions or other permanent positions successful? What were the opinions of others regarding your work? Did your university or college coursework reflect both a commitment to and an understanding of the content? Did the interview demonstrate your depth of knowledge of your discipline, of the developmental needs of students, of authentic ways to engage your learners? Did your professional portfolio provide evidence of your knowledge, skill, reflection, and capacity as an educator? Did your volunteer and other work experience broaden and enhance your capacity to work with others? These questions, and many more, provide applicants with opportunities to show evidence – evidence from multiple sources collected over time.

The broad collection of evidence supports the selection team in making the best possible decision given the context in which the applicant would be working. Just as whatever our students say, do, and create could be used as evidence of whether they have learned to the level of quality that we expect, an applicant's evidence of preparation and experiences supports a selection panel's decision-making (i.e., professional judgment) regarding an applicant's suitability for a position.

3. A Band Concert

Yet another way to think about the *during* and *at the end of* learning construct is to consider a band concert. Much preparation and practice is required before the very public display of a group's musicianship. In fact, it is like this: practice, practice, practice, practice, practice, and then it's showtime! Whether a concert sounds great, technically or artistically, is in direct relation to the opportunities to get it right during the practice time and to get specific feedback. The actual performance comes at the end of all that practice and is a result of that practice.

What connections might you make among these three examples? In schools across North America, experiences like these are replayed in classrooms daily. Are students penalized for their initial attempts? Is a full range of evidence used to determine a student's standing in a course? Do students have time to learn and get feedback to consider?

These examples remind us of the building blocks of quality classroom assessment. Students and teachers know what is to be learned; they collect evidence of learning from multiple sources over time; they understand and communicate quality and success; they have time to learn; they receive feedback; and they bring together evidence of learning that is collected to show all aspects of what needs to be learned. Then teachers make an evaluation decision – a professional judgment – after examining and considering all the evidence of learning. This is the process of classroom assessment.

> **What About...?**
>
> *This process of determining how well students are doing may make sense at the elementary level, but we are preparing our students for university or college. This may not work in the real world.*
>
> That students understand what needs to be done, how their current work compares to what is expected, and ways to close any gaps between the two are necessary skills that prepare them for the post-secondary environment, workplace success, and life beyond K-12 schooling.
>
> *(To read more about this, see What About I-1? on page 78.)*

Classroom assessment is a research-based inquiry process that has its roots in social science. Evidence of learning matters. As you work, it is important to take care when gathering evidence of learning for a particular course of study. When evidence of learning is collected from multiple sources over time (products, observations, and conversations), it is referred to as *triangulation* (Lincoln and Guba, 1984). And the evidence can be, potentially, as diverse as the students, teachers, and the various disciplines being taught. When evidence of learning is collected from multiple sources over time in relation to the learning destination, trends and patterns become apparent. This process can serve to increase the reliability and validity of teachers' professional judgment. Research clearly shows that teachers' *informed* professional judgment, in relation to a comprehensive collection of evidence, can be more reliable and valid than external test results (ARG, 2006; Burger et al., 2009).

To summarize the process of classroom assessment:

1. Informed classroom assessment is a set of methods and procedures that are grounded in research.
2. Evidence of learning is collected from multiple sources over time in relation to standards and is, potentially, as diverse as the students, teachers, and the various disciplines.
3. Teachers' informed professional judgment, in relation to comprehensive collection of evidence, collected with triangulation in mind, can be more reliable and valid than external test results.

▼ **Figure I-2**

Large-Scale and Classroom Assessment – What's the Difference?

	Large-Scale Assessment	Classroom Assessment
Purpose	To account for the achievement of groups of students in relation to the learning outcomes	To account for the learning and achievement of individual students
Research Question	What is the pattern and trend for groups of students at different points in the system?	Does this student know, apply, and articulate what he/she needs to know, do, and articulate given curriculum expectations?
Audience	The larger community as well as every part of the school system that works in support of student learning.	The primary audience is students and their parents with the secondary audience being the school and school system.
Reliability Your findings are repeatable – that is, they are collected over time day-by-day and you observe students creating evidence of learning. You actually witness students knowing, doing, and articulating what they need to know, do, or articulate over time.	Large-scale assessment has procedures to check for reliability.	Classroom assessment collects similar information (data) over time so that what a student knows, can do, and can articulate is evidenced through products, observations, and conversations.
Validity You are assessing what you are supposed to assess and the evidence of learning is collected from multiple sources over time (a process of triangulation).	Validity can be thought about in a variety of ways. Because of the amount of information collected through large-scale assessment, the findings are valid at the group level.	Validity, when it comes to classroom assessment, is often focused on the match of the evidence of learning to the learning expectations, as expressed in the relevant documents.

In conclusion, in each section of this book – preparing, engaging, and reporting – you, as teachers, will find the specifics of what needs to be done to successfully implement assessment, evaluation, and grading and reporting. There are numerous examples from a wide range of subject areas, including, for example, science, mathematics, social studies, English, English language learners, fine arts, physical education, vocational education, and music.

And, for those of you who work with teachers to create assessment plans and to implement them, this book complements *Assessment of Learning: A Professional Learning Resource on Standards-Based Grading and Reporting* (2008), a multimedia resource designed for people who support teachers and *Quality Assessment in High Schools: Accounts From Teachers* (2013), a book written by and for high school teachers. Having used the ideas in these two resources and fine-tuned them over the years, we know that they work.

> **What About...?**
>
> *At the high school level, there are high-stakes tests. So I can't afford to involve my students in this way.*
>
> If students know what is expected of them, if they know what their work should be like, and if they can self-monitor, they come to a deeper understanding of curricular standards and outcomes. They do better on external tests and measures.
>
> *(To read more about this, see What About I-2? on page 78.)*

This book is also meant for those of you in leadership roles: principals, assistant principals, district personnel, directors, and superintendents. It is important that you, too, understand these ideas. Your teachers need your support. They must believe that you "have their backs" as they do what is right for their students' learning.

And finally, we offer this advice: we can all use aspects of classroom assessment in our roles so that our work can be more practical, powerful, and possible.

That's it. It is as simple (and as complex) as that.

Let's get started.

CHAPTER 1

Preparing for Quality Classroom Assessment

"Students can reach any target that they know about and that holds still for them."

Rick Stiggins

CONTENTS

Determining the Learning Destination

Researching the Expected Quality Levels

Planning to Collect Reliable and Valid Evidence of Learning

Collecting Baseline Evidence of Learning

Whether you're planning a trip, searching for something online, teaching, or seeking to accomplish something else, reaching a destination is easier if you know where or what it is. That's the point Tyler (1949) was making over 60 years ago, when he said that the first question a teacher needs to answer is: What do I want my students to learn? In North America, the term *standards* or *learning outcomes* refers to that which students are expected to learn. It is also that by which their learning success will be judged.

Preparation for student learning just makes sense; if we don't know where we are going, we'll never get there. Taking time to determine just what we are required to teach – knowledge, understanding, application, and articulation – means that we can ensure that the evidence of learning we collect is what we need in order to ensure that our professional judgment is reliable and valid. Further, as we research the appropriate quality levels, we come to understand development over time and according to expectations. This means that we have the information we need in order to coach all students – wherever they are in their learning – towards success. As we review what needs to be learned and the quality levels expected, we begin to select the tasks, activities, assignments, and other evidence of learning that will provide both the learning opportunities and the evidence of learning needed in order to show learning. As we determine the kinds of evidence we might collect in terms of observations, products, and conversations, we also begin to see ways that we, as teachers, can collect the evidence of learning we need. This is also the time when teachers begin to consider what evidence of learning *students* can collect.

Preparation for student learning begins with preparing for quality classroom assessment. There are four areas to consider:

1. determining the learning destination
2. researching the expected quality levels
3. planning to collect reliable and valid evidence of learning
4. collecting baseline evidence of learning

1. Determining the Learning Destination

For most teachers, figuring out what standards or outcomes need to be taught (and learned by students) is harder than it sounds. It is not simply a matter of turning to the curriculum documents. Ideally, teachers need to be masters of their discipline; this is difficult when they are early in their careers or teaching outside their discipline and getting new teaching assignments each year. Whether teachers are masters of their discipline or not, they need to plan to be successful; they need to begin with the end in mind.

Consider this process (see Figure 1-1):

- Choose one subject area. You might want to think about one term, year, or semester.
- Download or copy the standards or outcomes that students are to learn and cut them into individual chunks. (This process helps you use more than just one of your senses, which is helpful in learning.)
- Organize the standards or learning outcomes into groupings that make sense to you by sorting the individual statements related to a topic, concept, or process.
- When the groupings are finalized, summarize each group by identifying a "big idea" so the standards or outcomes can be shared with others in simple, clear, student-friendly language that corresponds to how the learning needs to be reported later.
- Return and review the standards and outcomes in their original form. Check back to see if there is anything you've missed.
- Ask colleagues to review your draft using a protocol.
- Make revisions based on the results of the protocol conversation.

Figure 1-1 ▼

Deconstructing Curriculum Outcomes and Standards

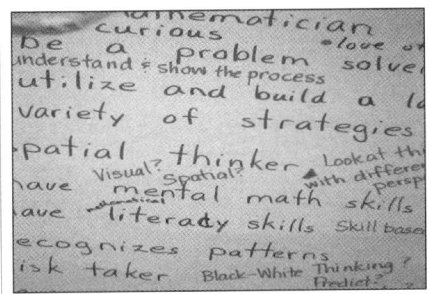

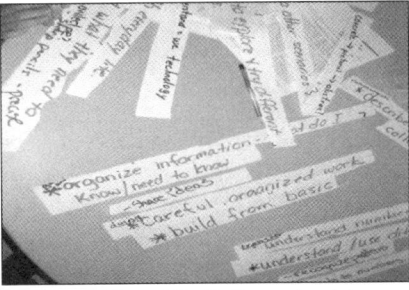

With a group of knowledgeable colleagues or on your own, analyze your curriculum and identify all key words and phrases. Then, group similar ideas together.

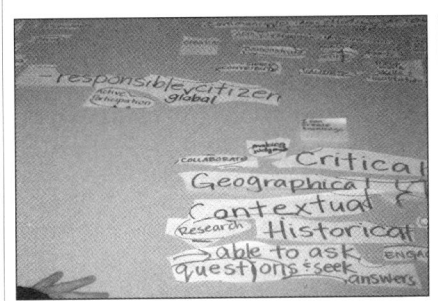

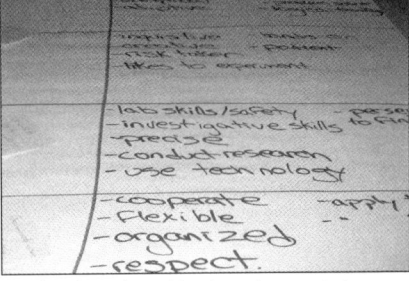

Create overall "big-idea" statements that will guide your planning and can be used to explain what students need to know, do, and be able to articulate.

With thanks to Anne Davies.

This is a deceptively simple process. It is important to group the standards or outcomes so you can see what parts can be taught together. This is an efficient way to proceed and will often enable you to address more than one standard or learning outcome in any given time period. This grouping will be unique to you and will reflect your understanding of your discipline. It is helpful to involve a trusted colleague to review your work and give comments about parts you might have missed or underemphasized.

Remembering and sharing four or five big ideas with others makes sense. Sharing 150 or more separate standards or outcomes is simply overwhelming for students, parents, and others. Teachers need to know all the standards and outcomes because they are responsible for teaching them. However, when teachers group standards and describe them in student-friendly language that describes quality, it helps everyone understand. This is

Figure 1-2 ▼

Learning Destination for English Language Arts

- Students read, view, and listen critically with understanding while making connections with self, with others, and with other experiences.
- Students write, represent, and speak thoughtfully for specific audiences, using a variety of forms.
- Students communicate and collaborate with others in small groups, in larger groups, and as part of a social online learning community.

Preparing for Quality Classroom Assessment

one of the first steps in preparing to teach students to monitor their own learning. (See Figures 1-2 and 1-3 for additional examples.)

Teachers engaged in this work need to take into account both what needs to be learned and how the learning needs to be reported. Descriptions of learning destinations vary from place to place because the contexts differ, and it seems that each jurisdiction has its own unique meanings for common terms. This work is made easier when teachers can work together across departments or grade-levels to draft student-friendly descriptions of learning destinations. As a result, teachers have more confidence and are better prepared to communicate with students, parents, and each other in the school community. Also, when draft versions of learning destinations are shared among faculty members, colleagues can improve and build upon the work. Everyone saves time while building confidence in the accuracy, clarity, and usefulness of the final drafts.

▼ **Figure 1-3**

Mathematics Standards and Student-Friendly Language

Standards Statements [1]	Student-Friendly Version
Know, understand, and apply the process of mathematical problem solving	• Know, understand, and apply the process of mathematical problem solving
Reason, construct, and evaluate mathematical arguments and develop an appreciation for mathematical rigor and inquiry	• Use mathematics to solve problems • Ask questions about mathematics • Think like a mathematician
Communicate mathematical thinking orally, in writing, and using a variety of representational forms	• Communicate mathematical thinking orally, in writing, and in other ways
Recognize, use, and make connections between and among mathematical ideas and in contexts outside mathematics to build mathematical understanding	• Recognize, use, and make connections between mathematical ideas • Make connections between ideas in mathematics and ideas outside of mathematics
Use technology as an essential tool	• Use technology to solve problems and learn more in mathematics
Demonstrate a positive disposition toward mathematical processes and mathematical learning	• Demonstrate a positive attitude toward mathematics

[1] Adapted from NCTM Standards

Once the standards and learning outcomes are grouped so they make sense, given their discipline and grade level, *and* teachers have summarized them so they make sense to their students, it is time to bring full meaning to the words. Teachers do this next step as they research the expected quality and achievement levels given grade expectations.

> **What About...?**
>
> *Secondary curricula are jammed with standards and expectations. I don't have time to do all of this with my students.*
>
> High school teachers who have involved students in their own assessment report that they save time – time that they could now spend with students who need additional instructional support. When students are clear about what is expected of them and about levels of quality, they can get right to the work. Students do not need to guess and teachers do not need, at every turn, to remind them about what they need to do.
>
> (To read more about this, see What About 1-1? on page 79.)

2. Researching the Expected Quality Levels

"What do you want?" asks a student. "How good is good enough?" asks a colleague. "What does excellence look like?" you wonder. These are questions that relate to the challenge of using standards or learning outcomes successfully to guide teaching, learning, grading, and reporting. Curricular standards or learning outcomes often define what students need in order to learn, be able to do, and be able to articulate *without* the document showing what it looks like when they do. For example, "communicates effectively in writing" looks different for a seven-year-old, a 16-year-old, or a 36-year-old. Teachers may know what the learning standard is, but they may need support to understand what it looks like for students of a particular age or in a particular discipline. And, if teachers are not clear about what reaching success looks like for their students, they will not know when their students have reached it.

Being able to recognize quality and success is an important part of professional judgment. There are ways that teachers can inform their professional judgment. For example, it is shown that comparing student work to samples or criteria improves teachers' professional judgment (ARG, 2006; Burger et al., 2009). Teachers can gather collections of samples that illustrate the standard or learning outcome from their work in progress, from collections available online, or from colleagues. When teachers analyze samples together using a protocol, they come to a better common understanding and collective agreement about quality expectations and achievement expectations for specific courses or grade levels.

It is true that teachers in the past learned informally about quality expectations as they worked with colleagues. However, in these times, teachers more and more often work together formally to share teaching expertise and to come to a common understanding of quality work. Conversations among colleagues are informed by:

- examining samples of student work for particular assignments or tasks

- looking at collections of student work to show development over time
- considering results of common assessments and performance tasks
- analyzing external assessment data

Looking at Samples of Student Work

Teachers work together to view samples, select those that best represent expected quality for assignments or tasks, and then go further to develop criteria. This process of identifying what is important in the work deepens their understanding of what quality is and what the expectations for a particular course or grade level are. Samples and exemplar collections can take many forms, including maps, reading responses, science lab reports, writing projects, evidence of mathematical problem-solving, videos of oral presentations, musical performances, computer animations, research projects – that is, anything that illustrates what students are expected to know, do, and can articulate in relation to their learning. (See Figure 1-4 for an example of teachers gathering and using samples.)

▼ **Figure 1-4**

ELA Teachers Gathering Samples
Example: Teachers were asked to collect samples of the great variety of texts students were using (viewing, reading, and listening) across all classes (fiction and non-fiction). Teachers gathered and examined the texts first of all in their department groups and then, later, in cross-department teams. They discussed what students would need to be able to do in order to understand and use the text. This information was gathered across schools and used to describe development in reading across curriculum areas.

Once teachers have determined which samples will best illustrate quality work and course or grade-level expectations, it is important that they continue to work together and create criteria with an accompanying rubric or a scoring guide. Teachers use the following questions to guide the development of rubrics:

- Does each level describe what success looks like? If it describes failure, how could it be rewritten?
- Does the language in each section describe what is working?
- Does the rubric describe what errors have been made? Can it be reworded so that it gives students quality feedback to guide their learning?
- Is the rubric easily understood by students? Parents? Colleagues?
- Does each level show the next steps for students? Are the steps appropriate?
- Are there work samples to illustrate the changes in quality from level to level?

From © 2004 *Facilitator's Guide to Classroom Assessment K-12* by Anne Davies

By using rubrics such as these, teachers engage in a process that informs their professional judgment; they are comparing their assessment of different samples of student work with their colleagues' assessments of the same samples. Talking with colleagues about differences in professional judgments gives everyone an opportunity to develop a shared understanding of what quality and expectations look like. (See Figures 1-5, 1-6a, and 1-6b for examples of two ways that mathematics teachers defined quality.)

Figure 1-5

Mathematics – Defining an `A` Text

A team of Grade 9 teachers met at the beginning of the school year and developed a description of success in Grade 9 mathematics. They deliberately included both qualitative and quantitative data because they collected evidence from multiple sources so all standards could be evaluated. They included the results of school-wide assessments, as well as the common assessments that their grade-level team had agreed upon. Each teacher also collected a range of evidence based on classroom work that had been designed to support each learner so it varied from student to student and class to class. In order to evaluate and to be clear to students and parents about how student learning in mathematics would be evaluated, the teachers developed criteria that described success. They also took time in their weekly planning sessions to review student work and, over the course of a year, created a collection of samples (based on student work) that represented the range of A-level work. Each teacher received a set of samples to use with students and parents. In addition, since each class had a range of students working at different levels, they researched developmental continua in the area of mathematics (problem-solving and numeracy) and began an inquiry project focused on mathematics development in the secondary years so they could assess for learning with more confidence.

Mathematics – Description of Letter Grade or Symbol

Student	Teacher	Evidence of Learning
I consistently and independently… • understand, remember, and apply mathematical concepts being studied • communicate my understanding of mathematical concepts • give everyday examples of use • solve problems using mathematical concepts, skills, and strategies to problems • work effectively by myself and with others • communicate effectively using words, symbols, and representations • connect ideas to self, to others, and to other ideas or tasks • use mathematical 'habits of mind' as outlined in the class criteria	[The student] consistently and independently… • understands, remembers, and applies mathematical concepts being studied • articulates a clear understanding of mathematical concepts and is able to give everyday examples of use • applies concepts, skills, and strategies to problems • analyzes problems, uses a variety of effective strategies to find possible solutions, and is able to check and evaluate the effectiveness of the process used • works effectively by self and with others • communicates effectively using words, symbols, and representations • connects ideas to self, to others, and to other ideas or tasks • uses mathematical 'habits of mind' including, for example, persistence, questioning, drawing on past knowledge, precision of language and thought	Evidence of learning collected over time from multiple sources demonstrates the student's learning by consistently and independently producing proof of learning. **Qualitative Data:** Proof of learning includes work collected over time: • products (e.g., work samples, tests, quizzes, common assessments) • observations (e.g., class work, demonstrations, performance tasks, teacher observations) • conversations (e.g., discussions, written reflections, journal entries, conferences, interviews) **Numerical Data:** • common assessment scores: (typically rubric scores of 4 and 5 on a five-point scale) • summative evaluations, such as performance tasks, projects, tests, and quizzes receive grades in the 91% - 100% range.

▼ **Figure 1-6a**

Mathematics Teachers Setting Criteria to Describe Quality

A group of mathematics teachers came together to discuss what quality was in relation to problem solving. They use the four-step process of developing criteria (Gregory, et al. 2011) to guide their conversations.

> **Co-Constructing Criteria:**
> **A Four-Step Process**
> Gregory, Cameron, and Davies (2011)
> *Setting and Using Criteria*, 2nd Edition
> 1. Brainstorm.
> 2. Sort and Categorize.
> 3. Make a T-chart.
> 4. Use it. Revise it. Use it again.

Because they were going to share the criteria with their students, they used language that was accessible and easily understood.

▼ **Figure 1-6b**

What counts when we solve a mathematical problem?

Brainstormed List
- explain solution using mathematical terms
- identify parts of the problem that are critical to arriving at the solution
- review and check my work
- have a sense of where to begin
- break the problem into steps and stages
- identify if something is missing that is necessary to solving the problem
- persevere – keep trying to solve the problem using different strategies
- attempt multiple ways of solving the problem
- make connections to similar problems
- use technology as needed

Criteria	Details
Understand the problem	• identify parts of the problem that are critical to arriving at the solution • have a sense of where to begin • identify if something is missing that is necessary to solving the problem
Choose a strategy to solve it	• persevere – keep trying to solve the problem using different strategies • attempt multiple ways of solving the problem • make connections to similar problems • use technology as needed
Describe how you reached a solution	• break the problem into steps and stages • explain the solution using mathematical terms • review and check work with a peer

Looking at Collections of Student Work

Teachers need to arrive at a well-informed professional judgment. Therefore it is important that they examine *all* the evidence of learning collected in relation to all the standards and learning outcomes upon which the report card grades are based. Looking at samples of just one or two pieces of student work is not good enough.

Collections of student work can be complex and can vary from student to student; therefore, teachers need to develop a common understanding of the many different looks of quality in relation to course or grade-level expectations and the expectations for a particular point in the learning. There are a variety of protocols available to inform this work (see Figure 1-7 for a sample).

Figure 1-7 ▼

SALT Protocol

A group of teachers worked together to redefine success in their classes. They moved from being grades-based on assignments, tests, quizzes, and participation to defining quality based on the evidence of learning in relation to course standards. Partway through the course, they asked students to review the evidence of learning that they had generated. Students put together the best collection of evidence they had that demonstrated that they were successfully meeting course outcomes. The teacher selected one student's collection of evidence that met the quality description. He brought it to the working session. As the colleagues gathered, they used a protocol that required a close examination of the evidence of learning. They commented on how it did (or did not yet) meet the quality expectations as defined. The presenting teacher was able to listen to his colleagues exercise their professional judgment in relation to the collection of evidence and consider how their comments were similar (or not).

Agreement about Quality

1. Appoint a timekeeper and facilitator. Begin.
2. The presenting teacher describes the evidence. (2 minutes)
3. Three reviewers ask questions to clarify. (3 minutes)
4. Group members review the work. They discuss the work in relation to excellence (e.g., A) while the presenting teacher listens. (5-7 minutes)
5. The presenting teacher joins the conversation and points out anything that might have been missed. (2 minutes)
6. Each participant sums up by commenting on where they think the evidence is in relation to excellence. (5 minutes)
7. The presenting teacher reflects on the process. The group reflects on the process. (5 minutes)
8. Repeat the process with another teacher presenting another body of evidence for one student.

© Copyright – Classroom Connections International Inc. www.connect2learning.com

Considering Results of Common Assessments and Performance Tasks

Teachers, schools, and school systems begin their work of considering results of common assessments by looking at the evidence of learning that they have agreed to have all their students create. This student work might be a performance task or a test, for example, or it might be a collection of student work from a unit of study that has the same learning goals.

Once the student work has been collected, teachers meet and co-construct criteria and the accompanying rubric (or scoring guide), focusing on what is important; they look at what is quality in a particular product or process that comprises part of the evidence of student learning. Teachers may choose to select anchor samples that illustrate key aspects of learning across the different levels of the rubric. Anchor papers of student work – work that serves as an illustration of the different levels of the rubric – are annotated so that they clearly communicate what part illustrates a particular level.

▼ **Figure 1-8**

Three Examples of Teacher Conversations about Assessments and Tasks to Inform Understanding of Quality

Example: *One jurisdiction asked teachers to join an action research project focused on exploring problem solving across all curricular areas. In teams they met in cross-curricular groups and discussed what problem solving looked like in their subject area. They gathered samples. They looked at samples gathered by other teams. They continued exploring problem solving in their classes during the year. Then, towards the end, they gathered the student samples together and built a visual rubric that documented growth in problem solving over time. They worked together to describe the key features in terms of what was important about the samples at each level. This became a draft rubric that they used in the following year to support student learning in terms of identifying what they were able to do and what they needed to do to improve.*

Example: *One jurisdiction developed a collection of samples that represented growth in the visual arts. A variety of media were represented in the collection. Teachers were asked to use the collection of samples to assess and provide support in terms of "next steps" for students and for their own teaching. Students also had access to the collection of samples along with teachers' annotations to support their growth and progress.*

Example: *A jurisdiction wanting to support local schools to engage in assessment that supported student learning launched an initiative to collect performance tasks in relation to the various curricular areas across high school core subjects. Each performance task had its purpose and link to the clearly articulated curriculum standards. Each task also had clear directions and a scoring guide, as well as samples of student responses to the tasks. Prior to posting them online, teacher teams acted as adjudicators to determine the quality of the student work. They examined the tasks and student responses for fidelity to the curriculum and principles of quality assessment. Once available, teachers were able to select key tasks that supported their own learning in the department and school and to assist in the assessment of students in their courses.*

Teachers then score the set of student work using the rubric (or scoring guide) and anchor samples to guide their decision-making. They record their scores privately using sticky notes or their own copies of the rubrics. Once they have finished scoring, they check for inter-rater reliability – that is, they look to see where their evaluations are similar and where they are different.

Where there are differences, they come to an agreement and, if needed, adjust the wording of the rubric to better reflect the intended meaning. This process of looking together at student work using a common task, test, or body of evidence of student learning is a helpful beginning point for understanding the key components of quality work. It is *not* the end of the process, however. If student learning stops here, informed professional judgment may continue to be elusive. It is important that teachers continue engaging in this process over time, continually checking for and further establishing common understandings of quality in relation to a particular grade level or subject area. (See Figure 1-8 for three examples of teacher conversations related to quality.)

Analyzing External Assessment Data to Inform Levels of Quality

The process of analyzing external test results provides teachers with an opportunity to consider where their students are experiencing success (and what they therefore want to continue doing or do more of) and to determine where students are struggling. For example, if teachers have determined what they feel are appropriate levels of quality and if they are making professional judgments of student work based on those levels of quality, they may determine that 90 percent of the students are meeting quality expectations.

Then, when the external test results arrive and they indicate, for example, that only 40 percent of students are meeting quality expectations, teachers have a choice. They could dismiss the external test as invalid or they could examine the test and see what was emphasized. They could ask themselves whether or not they need to adjust not only what they emphasize, but also the ways that students need to communicate their understanding and the quality level expected. This conclusion, in response to the question "Do our quality expectations match external expectations?" helps to inform and clarify. (See Figure 1-9 for questions that we have used successfully when considering the results of external assessment data.)

In summary, teachers' and students' future success can be thoughtfully supported through structured conversations, discussions, and learning. Over time, the result of these conversations is the development of commonly held levels of quality in relation to standards or learning outcomes. There are numerous resources to support this kind of work (e.g., DuFour, Eaker & Many, 2006; Glaude, 2005, 2010).

▼ **Figure 1-9**

Questions to Consider When Looking at External Assessment Data

Questions to use when analyzing external assessment data

1. What surprises you about the data?
2. What does not surprise you about the data?
3. What can this data tell us?
4. What does this data not tell us?
5. In what ways does this data represent this group of students?
6. In what ways does this data not represent this group of students?
7. How does this data compare to groups of students from this school in the past?
8. How does this data compare to the district average? State average? Provincial average?
9. We have put in place some interventions over the past year. This data tells us that what we have been doing is working well in these ways… is not working well in these ways…. What are some implications for action?
10. As we look at the data for our school over the past five years, we are doing better/worse/the same as before. What are your hunches about why this might be so?
11. What patterns and trends are emerging for you as you look at this data?
12. What patterns and trends are emerging for you as you look at the data over the past several years?
13. Specifically, what areas of strength are you noticing for this group of students?
14. Specifically, what areas of challenge are you noticing for this group of students?
15. What can we learn about what we are doing well as a department?
16. What can we learn about areas of challenge for us as a department?
17. What areas might we need to focus on in the next year/next semester?
18. Who might we need to enlist in order to more closely understand what this data is telling us?
19. What is this data telling us about sub-groups of our students (e.g., gender, ethnicity)?

3. Planning to Collect Reliable and Valid Evidence of Learning

The next part of developing an effective assessment plan is to identify potential activities, tasks, projects, and other learning opportunities – that is, evidence of learning. It takes some planning for teachers to make sure that they have enough evidence, the right kinds of evidence, and evidence that is reliable and valid. Teachers have a better chance of collecting reliable and valid evidence of learning when they deliberately use research methods that ensure proof of learning from multiple sources collected over time. Once teachers have drawn upon standards and determined what students need to learn, and have developed a sense of what success might look like for their students, it is time for them to consider what kinds of evidence of learning will need to be collected. This planning process not only informs instruction, but it also ensures validity and reliability. If teachers attend to validity and reliability while undertaking assessment in the classroom, then when it comes time to evaluate at the end of the learning period, they know that they have the evidence they need in order to make informed, high-quality, and accurate professional judgments. (See Figure 1-10 for more information about reliability and validity.)

Figure 1-10 ▼

Reliable and Valid Professional Judgment	
Your professional judgment is more reliable if…	Your professional judgment is more likely to be valid if…
• your findings are repeatable, that is, they are collected over time day-by-day and you observe students creating evidence of learning. • you actually witness students knowing, doing, and articulating what they need to know, do, or articulate over time.	• you are assessing what you are supposed to assess and the evidence of learning is collected from multiple sources over time (a process of triangulation).

Teachers can easily be overwhelmed by all the possible evidence of learning that they could be collecting in relation to the standards or learning outcomes. Think about the possible activities, tasks, projects, and other learning opportunities; the possible evidence of learning seems endless. And, if you consider the various ways that students might best show proof of their learning, the list gets impossibly long. How to make sense of it?

When teachers take time to plan the evidence of learning that they need in order to be confident that their evaluation is both reliable and valid, their work becomes manageable. Making a plan means considering the best evidence of learning at the classroom level, given your unique subject area and grade level. To be successful, you need a plan from the beginning, so that students can create the evidence and collect and record it. It is also important to be prepared to respond to the questions students often ask: "What counts? How much is it worth?"

Teachers often ask, "Given the standards and outcomes, what is the best evidence of learning? How much is enough?" The activities, tasks, projects, assignments, and tests that teachers plan in order for students to learn all that needs to be learned, given the standards and outcomes, determine the possibilities for students to show what they know, can do, and can articulate. Further, when teachers are seen to value all evidence of learning – both qualitative and quantitative – then students come to understand that everything they do, say, and create is potentially evidence of learning. This stance has the potential to change everything – from relationships, to motivation, to learning – because suddenly every moment, every action, every creation is of value. We evaluate what we value. What is valued then guides teaching and the collection of evidence of learning.

> **What About...?**
>
> *Tests and quizzes are the only way to make sure that our assessment is objective and fair. All this other stuff is too subjective.*
>
> Tests and quizzes are often viewed as objective, but, through their construction, elements of subjectivity result. Tests cannot measure everything that a curriculum demands that students do, create, and articulate. Instead, we need to ensure that our assessment and evaluation are reliable and fair. This builds equity, accuracy, and repeatability.
>
> *(To read more about this, see What About 1-2? on page 79.)*

When we begin with the end in mind and explain to students what they need to know, be able to do, and be able to articulate, we set students up for success. When teachers co-construct criteria or use samples to show a range or variety of acceptable work, they encourage students to represent what they know in different ways, while still being fair and equitable. For example, if the curriculum standard states that students should be able to "describe how human curiosity and needs have influenced science, impacting the quality of life worldwide," they could research and write about it, or they could draw a mind map and create a digital presentation with visuals that illustrate effect and change over time, or they could interview scientists to track questions that were starting points for scientific inquiry and map the impact of answers on people and environment, or they could use newspaper and magazine clippings to illustrate key ideas. The expected learning does not change, but what students can do to demonstrate their learning in relation to the standard can be different. This is a key concept for ensuring that all students show what they know using evidence of learning collected from multiple sources over time. Further, this process helps students come to know and use the language of assessment, which can then be used by students and others (e.g., educational assistants, student support teachers, parents) to give specific, descriptive feedback during the learning, so that they can self-monitor and self-regulate.

What is the effect of this thinking within a course of study? Here are two scenarios depicting how teachers can explain to students what counts at the beginning of the course:

> **Scenario 1:** *The teacher explains to students at the beginning of the course that what counts for their grades are three culminating assignments, a midterm, and a final test. The teacher makes this clear. Yet, suddenly the goal is no longer learning; rather, it is the culminating assignments and tests that the teacher has determined to be of value. In this class, it is likely that some students (teachers know which ones) will interpret this clear description as an opportunity to do as little as possible. "After all," they say, "as long as I turn in the culminating assignments and tests, I can fulfill my obligations." These students have understood the teacher's words (not their meaning) and will act accordingly. None of the other learning processes – engaging, asking thoughtful questions, debating ideas, and so on – count.*

> **Scenario 2:** *Let's repeat this scenario, this time knowing what we know about classroom assessment and evidence of learning. The teacher explains to students what they need to learn, know, do, create, and articulate in relation to the standards and outcomes. All these are detailed in the course outline. When students ask, "What counts? What is it worth?" the teacher responds, "Everything you do, say, or create counts. In this class what counts is learning. You will generate potential evidence of learning every moment of every day. You will make selections from the entire collection of evidence to best show your learning. This will include, but will not be limited to, tests and common assessments. You will use a folder to do that. And, at the end of the learning time, I will look at the evidence you have collected day-by-day, I will review my observations, and I will review interview notes and your journal notes and make a decision – an informed professional judgment – about your grade. If at any time you are unsure about how well you are doing, refer to the definition of quality work included in your course outline. It describes what the evidence of learning should look like, how much there should be, and the key attributes of quality. If you are producing enough quality products, if you are interacting with others in ways that show that you are learning, if you can talk about your learning in an informed way, then you will do well. Remember that everything – all evidence of learning – is of value because, potentially, everything is considered part of the evaluation."*

Think about the difference in these two scenarios. In the first one, the teacher may have to impose penalties for the students who choose to not attend classes or participate, or who turn in work late, for example. In the second scenario, students may not have the kind of clarity they are used to about the grading scheme (which sometimes enables those who choose to do as little as possible and still pass). But they do know that they are producing evidence of learning all the time that is being collected and will be examined. Which scenario reflects your classroom? Which scenario would you like to have in your classes? Which scenario is most likely to result in engaged students who learn? (See Figure 1-11 for a list of evidence across a term.)

▼ Figure 1-11

Evidence of Learning for One Term

English – Listening and Speaking Strand	Mathematics	Spanish as a Second Language
• speaker self-assessments • listener self-assessments • posters • PowerPoint presentations • reflection cards • peer listening logs • double-entry journals • e-journals • speaking proof cards • listening proof cards • scripted interviews • web pages • speaking and listening checklists (e.g., range of contexts, specific behaviours)	• tests • quizzes • math journal • assignments • performance tasks • group work interactions • self-assessments • problem-solving assignments • mathematical games • group talking • structured interviews • demonstration of math processes • four-pocket portfolio (I use mathematical language; I persevere; I apply math concepts to solve problems; I use technology in mathematics)	• response logs • oral reading • tests • quizzes • oral responses • small-group conversations • large-group conversations • narrative paragraphs • expository paragraphs • presentations • assignments • self-assessments • posters • role plays • story and text retellings • letters and emails

Once teachers plan the evidence that needs to be collected, they spend time thinking about who will collect what evidence of student learning and which samples or models will best support students in understanding the learning expectations.

As teachers become more knowledgeable about the implications of various theories of intelligence and ways of knowing, experience a greater diversity of students, and seek to meet the needs of the learners, they are expanding the ways that students show or represent what they know. It is essential that our assessment practices be equitable. It is also essential that our assessments be accurate reflections of learning. Treating students equally can be unfair. For example, when students are asked to represent what they know in social studies only in writing, some will be unable to do so because of their lack of skill as writers. However, when asked to demonstrate, illustrate, or to give an oral presentation, their knowledge and skill may rapidly become apparent (as will gaps in understanding). More and more teachers are introducing an element of choice into the form that products may take. For example, some teachers create a list of ideas with their students. Over time, as students learn more about various ways of representing their learning, the list grows. Consider the three general sources of evidence of learning gathered in classrooms: observations of learning; the products that students create; and conversations between teachers and students.

What About...?

We need to make sure that our assessment and evaluations are fair, and that means that we need to use all the same assignments, items, tests, and tasks to determine a grade or mark.

Success for all students – a frequently repeated phrase – requires differentiation. As adults, we can take different pathways to get to the same place or to get something done. Curriculum standards and outcomes tell us what students need to be able to do, say, and articulate; our curriculum documents do not provide a list of evidence that all students need to produce in exactly the same way. It is important that students provide us with evidence of learning of all the standards or outcomes in the curriculum. So we need to focus on giving students chances to learn and to show what they learned.

(To read more about this, see What About 1-3? on page 80.)

Observations of Learning

The list of evidence teachers plan to collect in relation to the standards or outcomes for a course or grade level needs to include the observations they will make while students are learning key processes related to the discipline being taught. Consider the standards or outcomes. Which of these can only be observed? This is what will need to be observed. And, the record of observations becomes evidence. Teachers might observe . . . formal and informal presentations, scientific method being applied, group or partner activities, planning and designing, persuading, giving opinions, following instructions, listening to others, arguing, predicting, communicating ideas to others, and the list could go on and on.

Observations made by the teacher are essential if classroom assessment and evaluation are to be reliable and valid. In addition to being necessary for triangulating the evidence of learning, some learning can only be observed. Some students are better able to show what they know by doing it; these "in-action" learners may record little in writing and therefore will need some of their learning assessed through teacher observation. Also, as products are constructed, teachers have opportunities to observe students' learning during the learning, not just at the end of learning. When there isn't enough observational evidence, evaluations at reporting time are at risk of being invalid because they are not corroborated through multiple sources over time. (See Figures 1-12 and 1-13 for examples of observations in geography and biology.)

Figure 1-12

Possible Observations to Show Evidence of Learning

Urban Spaces – A Geography Unit of Study

- use of Geographic Information System (GIS) software
- oral presentations that are appropriate for audience and purpose
- selection and use of appropriate tools and technologies to carry out research
- construction of graphs
- organization of information
- recording of information in appropriate formats
- clear articulation of perspectives
- student collaboration to achieve group goals and fulfill responsibilities
- listening skills (information, perspective, and understanding)
- understanding others' perspectives
- reaching consensus
- use and selection of primary and secondary sources of information
- articulation of issues, patterns, and generalizations
- skills in making decisions that reflect fairness and equity

Figure 1-13 ▼

Possible Observations to Show Evidence of Learning

Digestion and Nutrition – A Biology Unit of Study

- dissection skills during real or virtual dissections
- collaborating with others to achieve group goals and responsibilities
- attention and focus during demonstrations
- confidence to carry out investigations
- science lab skills
- attention to personal safety, the safety of others, and the environment
- appropriate selection and safe use of scientific equipment
- synthesis of information and the evaluation of the quality of sources
- interaction with and examination of data to identify its relevance, reliability, and adequacy

Collecting Products

Teachers collect various kinds of evidence to show what students can do in relation to the standards or outcomes for the course or grade level. These could include projects, assignments, notebooks, and tests. There are many ways for students to represent their learning, and, if we as teachers prescribe the evidence of learning, we may unnecessarily limit students' options to show what they know. (See Figures 1-14, 1-15, and 1-16 for different possibilities that represent learning.)

Figure 1-14 ▼

Some Possible Ways to Represent Learning

- draw a diagram
- make a timeline
- make a poster
- write a story
- build a web site
- do an oral presentation
- create an animated movie
- create or add to a Wikipedia entry
- build a model
- create a puzzle
- conduct a survey
- make a podcast
- produce a YouTube video
- make a recording
- do a report
- write a song
- interview people from other countries
- write a newspaper article
- create a song
- create a piece of visual art
- build a diorama
- write a play
- start and monitor an online discussion forum

▼ **Figure 1-15**

Possible Products to Show Evidence of Learning

Urban Spaces – A Geography Unit of Study

- paragraphs describing as well as comparing and contrasting rural, urban, and remote places
- graphic organizers to represent different urban, rural, and remote settlements
- admit and exit slips
- mind maps
- article analyses
- letters to community leadership
- field notes
- written responses to issues inherent in living in rural, urban, and remote places
- graphs and maps
- brochures
- persuasive writing
- research questions
- electronic presentations
- sort-and-predict frames
- reports

Figure 1-16 ▼

Possible Products to Show Evidence of Learning

Digestion and Nutrition – A Biology Unit of Study

- concept maps and frames
- exit slips
- science journals or notebooks
- science lab reports
- projects
- wellness portfolio
- instructional brochure
- demonstration notes
- observation notes
- biological drawings
- cloze exercises
- sort-and-predict frames
- written responses to questions
- tests and quizzes
- collections of scientific data

Conversations About Learning

Conversations between teachers and students may be face-to-face, via recordings, online, or in written form (such as self-assessments, journal entries, or conferences). For example, teachers listen to learners during class meetings and during individual or group conferences. They also listen to recorded self-assessments or read students' self-assessments. Teachers also have opportunities to "listen" when students assess their work in relation to criteria, analyze work samples for their portfolios, or prepare to report to their parents about their learning. As students think and explain, teachers listen, in order to gather evidence about what they know and understand in relation to the standards or outcomes for the course or grade level. Teachers can determine what students think about what they did or created; for example, students can talk about their best efforts, what was difficult or easy, what they might do differently next time, and what risks they take as learners. As students articulate their learning – as part of a reader's response, a mathematics response, or in some other way – they become better able to explain their thinking. The ability to explain their thinking is helpful not only during the day-to-day moments in the classroom, but also during tests, performance tasks, or external assessments. This kind of intellectual engagement helps students become self-regulated learners – that is, students who are able to learn and take effective action both in and out of school. (See Figures 1-17 and 1-18 for examples of conversations in a geography course and a biology course.)

▼ **Figure 1-17**

Possible Conversations to Show Evidence of Learning

Urban Spaces – **A Geography Unit of Study**

- self-assessment of students' skills to listen and express views and perspectives
- small- and large-group conversations that express informed and reasoned opinions
- group debriefing after external presentations
- oral presentations
- class conversations about the merits and issues of living in rural, urban, and remote places
- role plays of individuals' views in different communities
- written journal entries that capture student's conversation with self and document the stages of work towards the end-of-semester projects

Figure 1-18 ▼

Possible Conversations to Show Evidence of Learning

Digestion and Nutrition – **A Biology Unit of Study**

- self-assessment of dissection skills and lab skills
- class and small-group discussions about the digestive system
- self- and peer assessments of group processes used
- oral presentations
- use of scientific vocabulary and concept explanation
- eliciting, clarifying, and responding to questions, ideas, and diverse points of view
- reflections in science notebooks (conversation with self)

Remember that we build reliability and validity when we pay attention to collecting evidence of student learning across an extended period of time and from a variety of sources. In essence, we really are triangulating – that is, we are taking information from three sources over time. (See Figure 1-19, which shows how product, observation, and conversation pull together from the perspective of biology.) Each area repeats what has been highlighted in previous figures, but it is done this way in order to illustrate the complete body of evidence.

▼ **Figure 1-19**

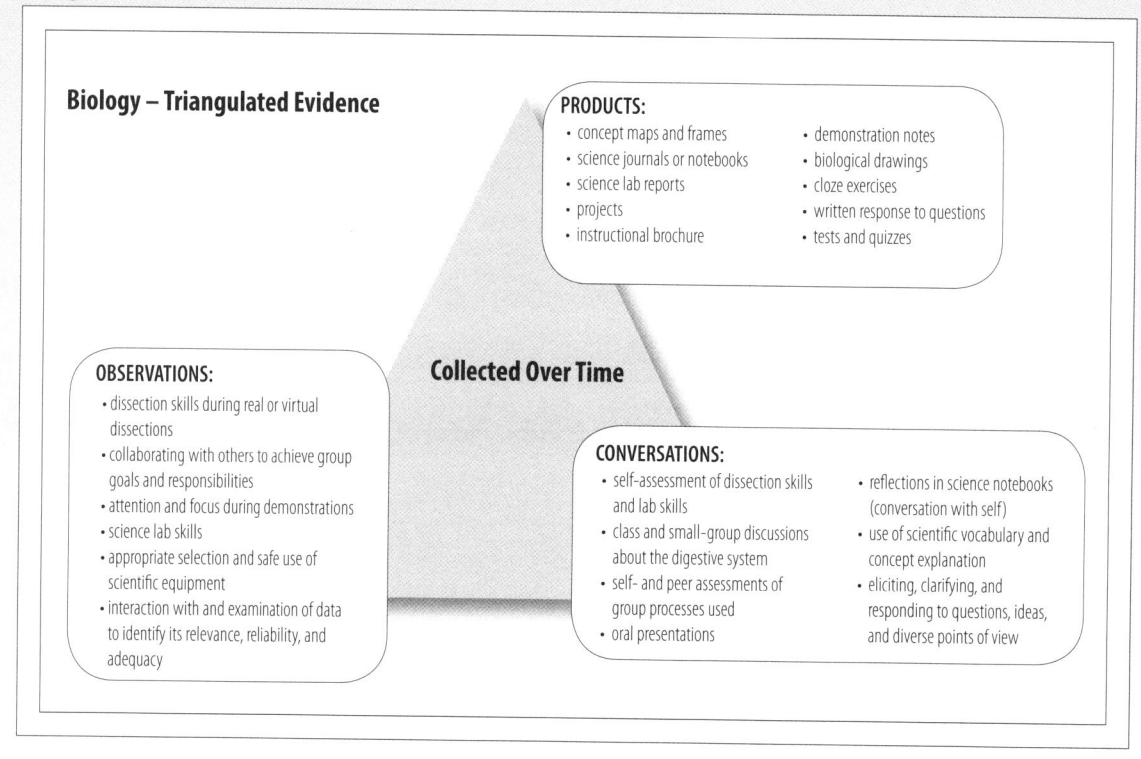

Biology – Triangulated Evidence

PRODUCTS:
- concept maps and frames
- science journals or notebooks
- science lab reports
- projects
- instructional brochure
- demonstration notes
- biological drawings
- cloze exercises
- written response to questions
- tests and quizzes

Collected Over Time

OBSERVATIONS:
- dissection skills during real or virtual dissections
- collaborating with others to achieve group goals and responsibilities
- attention and focus during demonstrations
- science lab skills
- appropriate selection and safe use of scientific equipment
- interaction with and examination of data to identify its relevance, reliability, and adequacy

CONVERSATIONS:
- self-assessment of dissection skills and lab skills
- class and small-group discussions about the digestive system
- self- and peer assessments of group processes used
- oral presentations
- reflections in science notebooks (conversation with self)
- use of scientific vocabulary and concept explanation
- eliciting, clarifying, and responding to questions, ideas, and diverse points of view

The next step in developing an effective assessment plan is to collect some baseline evidence of learning.

4. Collecting Baseline Evidence of Learning

As teachers collect products, conversations, and observations that provide evidence of students' learning, it is helpful for them to be able to demonstrate just how far students have progressed. That means that, early on in the learning, teachers collect evidence in critical areas so that the information gathered can later be used to compare students with their earliest levels of achievement. This type of evidence is often referred to as *baseline* evidence or baseline data. Because the term *baseline* is defined as "a minimum or starting point used for comparisons," collecting early evidence gives teachers a simple way to say "You used to . . . and now you . . ." or for students to say themselves "I used to . . . and now I . . ." For example, at the beginning of the biology unit *Digestion and Nutrition*, the teacher might observe students in a lab and note their scientific behaviours and engagement. The teacher might also collect and review a first lab report. In both these instances, the

Figure 1-20

Observations – at the beginning of the term, at the mid-way point, and at the end of the learning

Code:
(M) Consistently and Independently (WS) With Support and Reminders (NE) No Evidence at This Time

	Date:	Date:	Date:
Shows evidence of scientific 'habits of mind' (e.g., questioning, curiosity, perseverance, or precision of language and thought)			
Makes detailed observations			
Uses systematic approaches and scientific conventions			
Uses scientific vocabulary			
Uses equipment safely and for intended purpose			
Organizes data to assess patterns, trends, and relationships			
Uses scientific ideas in constructing explanations			
Works with others cooperatively and effectively			
Communicates effectively with others (in person, in print, in lab reports, and other forms of representation)			

teacher is paying close attention to and keeping track of how the students are performing early in their learning. This baseline data will not be used for summative purposes but will be considered later on in the semester in order to demonstrate how much the student has progressed in each of these two areas. As the course begins, the teacher identifies patterns and trends across the class, and she has a clear idea about areas of strength and areas for instructional direction. (See Figure 1-20 for an example of an observation frame for scientific behaviours and engagement.)

▼ **Figure 1-21**

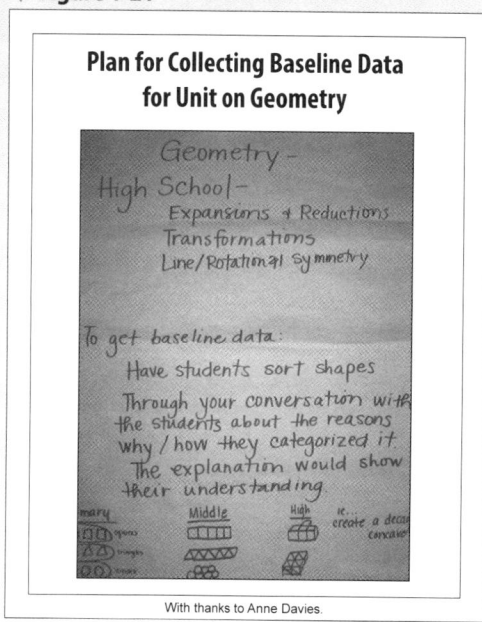

Plan for Collecting Baseline Data for Unit on Geometry

Geometry –
High School –
Expansions + Reductions
Transformations
Line/Rotational Symmetry

To get baseline data:
Have students sort shapes
Through your conversation with the students about the reasons why/how they categorized it
The explanation would show their understanding.

With thanks to Anne Davies.

In the geography unit, *Urban Places*, the teacher may ask students to write a reaction to an issue related to a particular topic. Additionally, he may observe students in conversation, applying criteria that describe effective small-group dialogue. These two types of evidence are critical, as students will be responding in both written and oral form to current events and issues throughout the semester. As he reviews the student work and the data that was collected, the teacher's next instructional steps surface. Later on in the semester, students will compare their first written attempt to the criteria that have since been constructed and to their growing understanding of the critical elements of an effective written response. As students look back at previous work, they can make statements of progress backed up with evidence from their own work. (See Figure 1-21 for an example of baseline data in geometry.)

In summary, teachers deliberately plan to collect a range of evidence – both qualitative and quantitative data – matching it to the curriculum standards for which they are responsible. They look at the learning destination and respond to some simple questions about both what will be collected and how it is going to be collected. Different teachers collect different kinds of evidence of learning, even though the description of what their students need to learn may be the same. This is so because the learning experiences that teachers design for different groups of learners may vary. Also, since students learn in different ways and at different rates, collections of evidence may vary in terms of how students choose to represent their learning. When making lists of the evidence they collect, teachers need to make sure that they plan to gather evidence from a variety of sources and that they gather evidence over time. (See Appendix B for some planning questions to help guide your work.) Remember that all students must have equal opportunities to show proof of learning regardless of how they learn, how they show their learning, or whether or not (or how much) they struggle.

> **What About...?**
>
> *Being involved in their own assessment makes sense when teachers are working with students who "get it." It just does not work with students who struggle.*
>
> Students who struggle are often the ones who can't figure out intuitively what is expected of them. It is, therefore, important to help those students to know and understand what is expected, what the work looks like when it is done well, and ways that they can determine where their work lies in terms of quality.
>
> *(To read more about this, see What About 1-4? on page 81.)*

Now that you have planned to let your students and others, like their parents, know what is expected of them, what the levels of quality are, the kinds of evidence that need to be produced, and the ways in which evidence will be collected, it is time to take action. In the next chapter – Activating and Engaging Learners – we describe in four easy steps just how you can do just that:

1. describing the learning destination and expected quality
2. involving students and providing time and support for them to learn
3. teaching to student needs based on assessment evidence
4. collecting reliable and valid evidence of learning

CHAPTER 2

Activating and Engaging Learners Through Quality Assessment

CONTENTS

Describing the Learning Destination and Expected Quality

Involving Students and Providing Time and Support for Them to Learn

Teaching to Student Needs Based on Assessment Evidence

Collecting Reliable and Valid Evidence of Learning

"Innumerable classroom events enable teachers to gather information about pupils by observing, questioning, listening to informal discussions, and reviewing written work. In formative assessment, this information may be used immediately to help pupils or it may be stored and used to plan future learning opportunities. . . . For formative assessment, the evidence is interpreted in relation to the progress of a pupil towards the goals of a particular section of work. Next steps are decided according to what has been achieved and what problems have been encountered. The interpretation is framed in terms of what to do to help further learning, not what level or grade a pupil has reached."

Assessment Reform Group (2006, pp. 9,10)

Attending to standards-based grading and reporting *during* the learning makes sense for five reasons:

1. The primary purpose of assessment and evaluation is to support learning. Students who are engaged, motivated, and have a sense of ownership are more likely to learn.

2. The secondary purpose of assessment is to communicate and report that learning to others. Students know what needs to be learned and who understand quality can self-monitor their way to success, collect evidence of learning, and explain to others why the evidence is proof of learning can be partners in the classroom assessment process.

3. If teachers are to collect what they need for evidence of learning at the end of the learning time, they need to ensure its creation and collection *during* the learning. Having students involved in collecting evidence of learning in relation to learning goals means that it is more likely that teachers will have more powerful and comprehensive collections of evidence of student learning.

4. Considering standards-based grading and reporting during learning makes sense also from a research perspective on learning (Crooks, 1988; Black & Wiliam, 1998; Looney, 2005), engagement (Stiggins, 2013), motivation (Butler, 1988; Covington, 1998; Harlen & Deakin Crick, 2002; Reay & Wiliam, 1999; Roderick & Engel, 2001) and the reliability and validity of teacher evaluation of student learning (ARG, 2006; Burger et al., 2009; Gordon & Reese, 1997).

5. Classroom assessment is a kind of research undertaking. Teachers must be present for the ongoing learning process in order to be witnesses to it. The result is that, by the end of the learning, teachers can say with confidence, "Look at the evidence. It is clear. This is what the student has learned."

What About...?

Only test scores and marks motivate students. We need to give them more of that. They need that kind of information.

Some students can decode what a 98 percent or a 57 percent means. But for most students, especially those who struggle, the 57 percent does not tell them what they did well and what they need to do differently. Motivation is built upon a foundation of understanding what needs to be done and believing that one has those competencies and skills (Butler, 1988; Covington, 1998; Gordon & Reese, 1997; Harlen & Deakin Crick, 2002; Pink, 2009; Reay & Wiliam, 1999; Roderick & Engel, 2001).

(To read more about this, see What About 2-1? on page 82.)

Assessment *for* learning – formative assessment plus the deep involvement of learners in the assessment process – is a powerful *instructional* tool. Black & Wiliam (1998) summarize their research findings by concluding that assessment *for* learning has the most powerful effect on student learning of any innovation *ever documented*. Teachers who want to have this kind of powerful effect use assessment *during* the learning to engage, motivate, and inspire students.

Consider the following nine actions that teachers can take to support, engage, and motivate learners in an environment of increased testing pressure. They are detailed in the Assessment Reform Group's *Testing, Motivation, and Learning* (Harlen & Deakin Crick, 2002, p. 8). The authors state that research shows that teachers need to "do more of this:"

1. Provide choice and help pupils to take responsibility for their learning.
2. Discuss with pupils the purpose of their learning and provide feedback that will help the learning process.
3. Encourage pupils to judge their work by how much they have learned and by the progress they have made.
4. Help pupils to understand the criteria by which their learning is assessed and to assess their own work.
5. Develop pupils' understanding of the goals of their work in terms of what they are learning; provide feedback to pupils in relation to these goals.
6. Help pupils to understand where they are in relation to learning goals and how to make further progress.
7. Give feedback that enables pupils to know the next steps and how to succeed in taking them.
8. Encourage pupils to value effort and a wide range of attainments.
9. Encourage collaboration among pupils and a positive view of each others' attainments.

Engagement in learning is directly connected to students' use of cognitive, meta-cognitive, and self-regulatory strategies that monitor and guide the learning process. When students are involved in the assessment process – examining samples, co-constructing criteria, self-assessing, collecting evidence of their learning, and communicating it to others –

they are engaged in meaningful ways. In this chapter we will describe what teachers need to *deliberately* and *intentionally* do in order to capitalize on the documented power of assessment to support student learning. There are four classroom assessment functions that teachers can engage in to activate and engage learners:

1. describing the learning destination and expected quality
2. involving students and providing time and support for them to learn
3. teaching to student needs based on assessment evidence
4. collecting reliable and valid evidence of learning

1. Describing the Learning Destination and Expected Quality

When teachers inform and involve students (and parents), when they know from the beginning what is needed in order to be successful, students learn more. Research highlights the importance of helping students picture quality and success. No wonder. Think about it. When teachers and students know where they are going, they are more likely to achieve success. Once students know what they are supposed to be learning, they can self-monitor, make adjustments, and learn more. That is why teachers talk about the learning destination in student-friendly language (see Figures 2-1 and 2-2), provide information about the relevance of the learning to their lives in and out of school, show samples and criteria to help learners understand quality and success, and identify potential evidence.

▼ **Figure 2-1**

Learning Destination Written in Student-Friendly Language	
Mathematics	*Food from the Land* – A Social Studies Unit of Study

• I show an appreciation and value for mathematics.
• I solve problems in multiple ways.
• I make connections to life, other subjects, and mathematical concepts.
• I communicate using mathematical vocabulary and language.
• I develop and apply new mathematical knowledge.
	• I know about and can tell others about:
	  ◦ issues related to food production
	  ◦ conditions that are required for food to be produced
	  ◦ how food is produced
	  ◦ safeguarding our food supply
	• I manage information and ideas.
	• I think critically and creatively.
	• I communicate my thoughts and ideas to an audience.

Figure 2-2 ▼

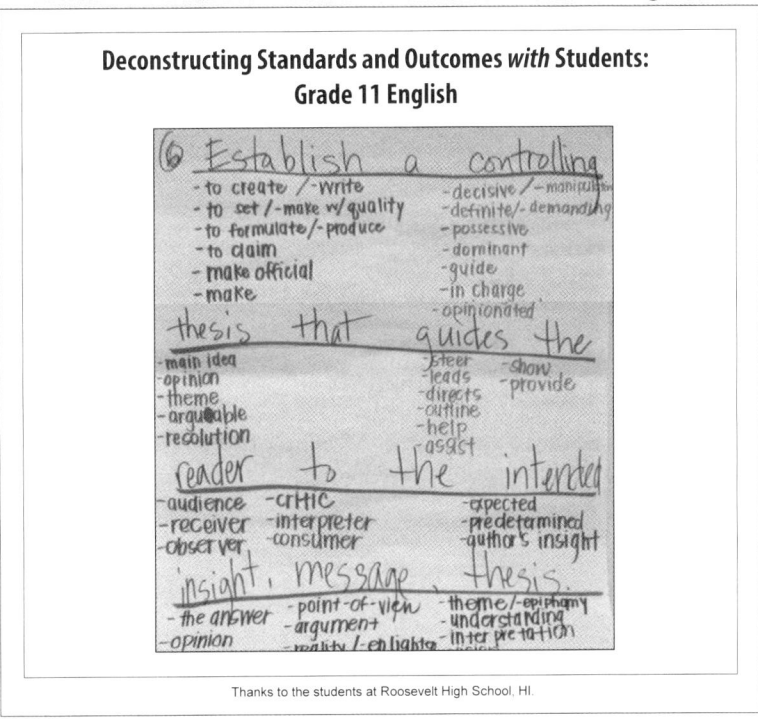

**Deconstructing Standards and Outcomes *with* Students:
Grade 11 English**

Thanks to the students at Roosevelt High School, HI.

Whether the standard has to do with writing or applying an equation, the learning dictates the form of the evidence. For example, if the curriculum standard or learning outcome states that students should be able to "describe the difference between mitosis and meiosis," there are multiple ways that they could show what they know. And, when they show what they know, the learning expectation doesn't change. What the student does to demonstrate progress towards that standard might be different from what another student does. Both would have provided evidence of learning.

Then, as teachers talk with students about what counts – evidence of learning – they share samples that illustrate a range of possibilities. They share or co-construct criteria for products, process, and collections of evidence so that the expected learning is explicit and learners can confirm, consolidate, and integrate new knowledge. In order to identify what quality and success can be, students look for what is common among the samples and the criteria. This process scaffolds future learning and helps teach about quality expectations. Also, the process of co-constructing criteria assists learners to understand and use the language of assessment to self-regulate and to self-monitor. (See Figures 2-3 and 2-3a for examples of co-constructed criteria and a list of potential samples.)

▼ Figure 2-3

Assessment of a Seminar Performance

Students, working with their teacher, agree to:

- demonstrate a high degree of understanding of content
- consistently encourage the participation of others
- consistently listen
- independently contribute personal perspectives
- share experiences
- consistently reference the ideas of others

While he observed students in seminar discussions, he notes that the addition of an online discussion led to a "portfolio of evidence that can be referred to in one-on-one conversations as well as a ready supply of exemplars for assessment" (Mindorff, 2013, pp. 167-168).

▼ Figure 2-3a

Examples of the Use of Samples and Criteria to Show Quality

Choral Course	Mathematics
<ul><li>examples of performances from videos, DVDs, and YouTube</li><li>co-constructed criteria on successful singers and performers</li><li>co-constructed criteria on powerful performances</li></ul>	Examples of *Criteria*<ul><li>classroom norms</li><li>group discussions</li><li>problem-solving</li></ul>Examples of *Modelling*<ul><li>use of technology</li><li>math experiments</li></ul>Examples of *Rubrics*<ul><li>exam — constructed response</li><li>journals</li></ul>Examples of *Student Work*<ul><li>assignments</li><li>journals</li><li>review sheets</li></ul>

Though we do not combine grades for achievement (in relation to outcomes) with grades for attitude, effort, work habits, or participation, we do know that there are habits of mind or learning skills that support students in their progress and growth. Teachers need to be just as clear about expectations for quality work habits or learning skills as they are for achievement in relation to outcomes, even though these may be reported to parents in a different section of the report card.

For example, a group of guidance counsellors worked with a group of tenth-grade students who were at risk of leaving school early. Part of their time together was allocated to looking more closely at what it meant to be a team member, to work independently when required, to self-regulate, and to collaborate. After discussion, students and teachers co-constructed criteria in these four areas. (See Figure 2-4 for both the brainstormed list and the criteria that were agreed upon by the teachers and the students as they worked and learned together.)

Figure 2-4 ▼

What Counts in Collaboration?

Brainstormed List

- understands the task
- uses respectful language
- minimizes negative expressions
- attends
- is punctual
- participates in discussion
- is prepared
- listens to the ideas of others
- listens to the concerns of others
- cooperates
- compromises as necessary
- fulfills the assigned role within the group
- reflects on work
- does a share of the work
- responds positively to others
- builds relationships with others
- works towards the goal
- stays on task
- works to resolve conflict
- shares information
- does not "put down" others

Criteria	Details
Communicates in a positive way	• uses respectful language • minimizes negative expressions • listens to the ideas of others • listens to the concerns of others • responds positively to others • does not "put down" others
Understands and stays focused on the task	• understands the task • attends • is punctual • is prepared • fulfills the assigned role within the group • does a share of the work • works towards the goal • stays on task • shares information
Engages with others cooperatively	• participates in discussion • cooperates • compromises as necessary • reflects on the work • builds relationships with others • works to resolve conflict

2. Involving Students and Providing Time and Support for Them to Learn

We can't just tell students what they need to learn and what their learning needs to look like. Just as teachers need to know what students know, can do, and can articulate, students also need to know *for themselves* what they know, can do, and can articulate. The strategies and structures that teachers use need to be simple, practical, and possible to do in busy classrooms. It is important for teachers to provide as much time as is possible, given reporting requirements and instructional time constraints and for students to be involved, to give and receive specific and descriptive feedback, and to create and have a role in providing evidence of their learning. Teachers seeking to involve students in classroom assessment engage students in:

- co-constructing criteria around process or products
- analyzing samples of student work
- undertaking self- and peer assessment
- setting meaningful goals
- collecting evidence of learning
- reflecting, selecting, and communicating proof of their learning to others

Students used to receiving evaluative feedback – right, wrong, 65 percent, or 92 percent – may need time to come to appreciate their role in the assessment process and learn how to self-monitor, self-assess, and regulate their own actions. For example, students learn to self-regulate and to self-monitor by using samples and co-constructed criteria. When teachers scaffold student self- and peer assessment in this way, both teachers and students see the power of assessment to support learning, to engage, and to motivate. These processes help students give themselves and others timely and specific feedback. (See Figure 2-5 for some ideas for specific, descriptive feedback from teachers to students and for some ideas from student to self, see Figure 2-6). In this way, learners, whether teachers are present or not, have an opportunity to figure out what they know and what they need to learn next. They can take stock of where they are in relation to where they need to be if they are to be successful. This ensures that learners have the information they need to adjust so they can continually improve the quality of their work in relation to standards and more specific learning expectations. In summary, when teachers deliberately share the purpose of self-assessment (see Figure 2-7 on page 36) with their students, the students learn more.

Figure 2-5 ▼

Ideas for Specific, Descriptive Feedback from Teachers to Students

In Relation to Co-Constructed Criteria	Teachers can use criteria with columns that have the following headings: Met, Not Yet Met, I Notice...
Sample Match	Teachers compare student work with samples that have been shared and are posted.
Using Class Codes	Teachers can assign codes such as triangle (quality is better than last work), squiggle (quality is the same as last work), question mark (quality is not as good as last time).
Practice, Practice, SHOWTIME	Teachers let students know they will have three opportunities to "show what they know." They get specific feedback to support learning and improvement. Then, when it is time, they choose which one "counts" for evaluation.

▼ Figure 2-6

Ideas for Specific, Descriptive Feedback from Student to Self

Once students have experienced specific, descriptive feedback in relation to co-constructed criteria, they can begin to give themselves specific, descriptive feedback in relation to that criteria.

In Relation to Co-Constructed Criteria	Students can use criteria with columns that have the following headings: Met, Not Yet Met, I Notice...
Sample Match	Students compare their work to samples that have been shared and are posted.
Using Class Codes	Students assign codes such as triangle (quality is better than last work), squiggle (quality is the same as last work), question mark (quality is not as good as last time).
Practice, Practice, SHOWTIME	Students know they will have three opportunities to "show what they know." They give specific feedback to support their learning and improvement. Then, when it is time, they choose which one "counts" for evaluation.

▼ **Figure 2-7**

Transcript from Social Studies — William Grindell

Grade 10 social studies teacher explaining to his students why self- and peer assessment are relevant for them in their lives:

"[Self-assessment] is a very important skill for you to learn. . . . Some of you are planning to go to college, and others will be entering the work force. When a professor says to you, "Here is a project. It is due at the end of the semester and it is going to be 50 percent of your grade," he will usually give you a list of criteria. When you deliver that project, you want to know for yourself if you are going to get an A or a B. You want to know if you are going to pass the course. The way you are going to know that is by assessing your own work. Looking at the criteria the teacher gave you, look to see if your project matches, and if it doesn't, you have a chance to fix it before you turn it in. It is only going to improve your work. Or, if you are going into the work force, imagine that your boss says to you, "Harrison, tomorrow I need you to do a presentation for our clients," and you are going to have to put together the presentation. You don't want to go to your boss and say, "Do you think this is good work or not?" or "Do you think this is going to be a good presentation?" You should be able to assess your own stuff."

William Grindell, *Assessment for Learning K-12*, Davies, 2010.

Another account that illustrates the connection between criteria and goals comes from a secondary history classroom. The teacher pulled together a group of four students. They met to provide feedback to each other about their individual research papers on the similarities and differences between pre-Colonial life and life today. Students used the criteria that they had co-constructed after reviewing high quality reports from past years. Before giving peer feedback, the students read each other's reports. They then identified the criteria that were met in the work and the criteria that were not yet present. Students made one comment in each area and then gave the criteria sheets back to their peers (see Figure 2-8). The teacher used this as an opportunity to get a "temperature check" regarding students' understanding of how to write a report, as well as a chance to observe their skill in providing specific, descriptive feedback. The information that the teacher gathered helped her to plan lessons for the next two class periods.

Figure 2-8

Important Components of a Dialectic Research Paper

What is important about a dialectic research paper?

Success Criteria	Details/Specifics	Met	Not Yet Met
Make sure it is organized and in the proper format.	• format MLA • works cited from legitimate and published sources • multiple sources • neatness • order/structure • intro to pro side and end with blunt clear statement		
It must have relevant content.	• different kinds of sources • using expert opinion • pictures/visuals • statistics • multiple forms of research-interviews, books, news • evidence examples		
Stay on topic and express both perspectives.	• need to make the argument • balance both perspectives • get point across • quotes or summary of expert opinion • factual information • understand point of view • understand motivations • long enough • no unnecessary information		
Clearly prove your point (include a clear thesis and conclusion).	• voice the argument • arrive at your own conclusion • clear thesis statement • firm conclusions • establish points clearly		

© 2012 Anne Davies connect2learning

Setting specific, attainable goals is more possible when students have been engaged in co-constructing criteria for any product or process important to the class or the discipline. Goals become more specific and attainable if students identify the aspects of their work in relation to co-constructed criteria that are not yet met or do not yet match the samples or criteria. Through the use of samples and criteria, they make such statements as "I need to be able to pick out key information in word problems and decide which math operations make sense and why" instead of identifying broad goals like "I need to get better at math." (See Figure 2-9 for an example from English language arts.)

▼ Figure 2-9

Highlighting Criteria

When students have criteria for a specific assignment, goal setting can be straightforward. We ask our students to highlight any criterion that they did not meet. This criterion becomes their short-term goal (see below).

Criteria for Oral Presentation	Details/Specifics
- Interesting to an audience	- look interested in your subject - make it interesting - keep it short
- easy to follow	- ==use small cards for notes== - slow down - use specific examples to get your point across - make sure you have a conclusion - we need to know what your topic is right away
- speech and manner help the audience listen	- ==look up at your audience== - have to be able to hear you - no fidgeting - stand straight

Adapted from Gregory, Cameron, Davies, *Self-Assessment and Goal Setting*, 52

In summary, we give students time to learn and time to "get it right" by helping them understand the learning destination, by co-constructing criteria around process or products, and by involving them in analyzing samples of student work. Then, as they create evidence of learning, teachers engage students in self- and peer assessment and goal setting in relation to the criteria that they have helped to construct. As the learning proceeds, teachers ask students to collect specific evidence of learning in relation to the learning destination. Teachers also collect evidence of their learning. Then, towards the end of the learning time, students are supported in reviewing the evidence they have collected, in reflecting, and then in selecting proof of their learning. Lastly, they communicate their evidence of learning to others.

> **What About...?**
>
> *At the secondary level, I might see over 130 students in a semester. There is no time for me to do this.*
>
> Involving students means that they are more actively involved and do things that the teacher has traditionally done alone. Helping students to clearly know what is expected, what quality looks like, and ways that they can give themselves and others specific and descriptive feedback frees up time for the teacher to work with those students who need directed and specific help.
>
> *(To read more about this, see What About 2-2? on page 83.)*

This process ensures that students receive specific and descriptive feedback from themselves, their peers, and their teachers. It gives students time to learn before receiving evaluative feedback. In this way, based on the specific, descriptive feedback received, students can move their learning forward – that is, students, with their teachers' support, learn to adjust and refine in order for their work to become more closely aligned with what is expected of them.

> **What About...?**
>
> *It does not make sense to allow students the opportunity to re-do their work. They should have only one chance, and that is all.*
>
> The real world provides us with many second chances – getting our diplomas in our 40s or re-taking our driver's license test, for example. We work with students and provide them with specific and descriptive feedback so they can produce work that more closely aligns with the curriculum and our expectations.
>
> *(To read more about this, see What About 2-3? on page 83.)*

3. Teaching to Student Needs Based on Assessment Evidence

Feedback is important for students. But it is equally important for teachers, who are in a position to adjust their strategies to meet the needs of and gaps in students' learning. Teachers use the process of *formative assessment* to guide their deliberate planning for each student's success. During this process, teachers determine what students know, can do, and can articulate. Next, they compare the learning with what students need to know. Then they *deliberately plan* ways to close the gap for each learner. This process is continuous, as teachers collect evidence of learning moment-by-moment in their classrooms. In order to engage in formative assessment successfully, teachers:

- routinely collect and use baseline data in relation to key concepts and processes prior to planning for learning and implementing the instructional sequence.

- assess what students know, can do, and can articulate during the instruction, based on the evidence of what has been learned and what has not yet been learned.

Teachers accomplish the steps in this process in various ways, depending on the discipline and grade level in which they are working and on their own personal preferences. For example, many high school teachers collect evidence of student learning and progress at the beginning of the semester, at mid-semester, and at the end of the semester. This evidence proves, in an authentic manner, the ways in which a student's work and learning grows over the semester and identifies instructional pathways. For example:

- The chemistry teacher gathers lab reports from students at the beginning, middle, and end of the semester.

- The band teacher has students play selected pieces of music at the beginning, middle, and end of the semester. The performances are recorded, and the results are attached to students' self-assessments and posted.

- The English literature teacher collects students' expository writing samples that compare a published text to their current work. He does this at the beginning, middle, and end of the semester.

- Students in a high school Spanish class digitally record themselves describing what they did on the weekend. These files are stored electronically at the beginning, middle, and end of the semester and are kept to refer to at the culmination of the course.

As teachers consider the evidence at these three critical times, they come to better understand patterns and trends in student learning and achievement. This, in turn, helps them plan instruction.

With the information gathered at these critical times, teachers can target what instructional next steps need to be taken for the group, as well as for specific sub-groups or individuals; they also know which groups of students may require additional support. Consider these examples:

Example 1: *A high school mathematics teacher has students use small personal whiteboards. As he provides students with instruction in a particular concept, he has students work through an algorithm or problem on the whiteboard. He walks around the classroom looking over the students' shoulders to notice what they are doing well and where they are struggling. He then returns to the front of the classroom and carries on with instruction that tightly fits the needs of the students at that very moment.*

Example 2: *An industrial arts teacher has shared the criteria that specifically described what safety looks like in his lab. As he observes the students, he writes down the initials of the students who are meeting the criteria and those who are not yet meeting them. At the beginning of the next class period, he gathers the students whom he had noted were not yet meeting some of the required criteria and does a quick mini-lesson highlighting the safe use of the power tools.*

The next part of working with students *during the learning* is to have them collect the evidence of what they know, what they can do, and what they can articulate.

4. Collecting Reliable and Valid Evidence of Learning

There are endless ways for both teachers and students to collect triangulated evidence of learning. It is important that teachers find the ways that suit them. Here are two examples of ways that teachers find useful:

> **Example 1 Observations:** *A high school biology teacher has over 90 students per term. In his assessment plan (see Figure 2-10) he has noted the need for observing how students are working in the lab setting. However, he must make it manageable with this number of students. He has four criteria for effective lab work in biology: (1) active student involvement (S); (2) correct use of lab equipment (L); (3) appropriate experimental design (D); and (4) recording data and observations (R). For each lab, he has a class list with each of these acronyms beside each student's name (see Figure 2-11). As he observes students at work, he circles or highlights the criteria (the letter) that he sees students demonstrating. Each day he records the date in the colour of ink he is using for recordkeeping; he can see patterns and trends over time and then determine the next instructional steps. (See additional examples in Figure 2-12.)*

▼ **Figure 2-10**

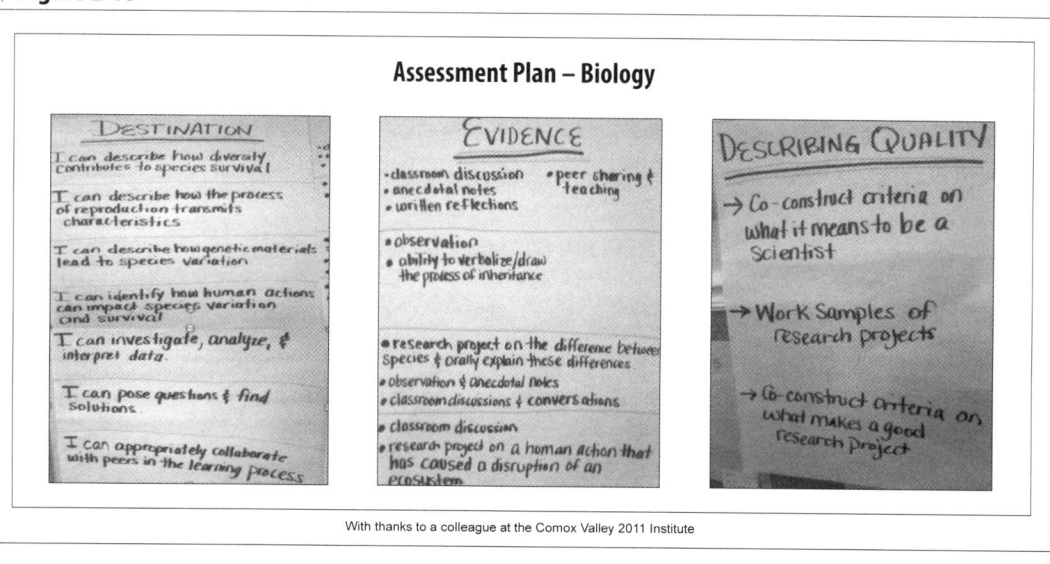

Assessment Plan – Biology

With thanks to a colleague at the Comox Valley 2011 Institute

Figure 2-11

Recording Observations in a Biology Class

Names	Date 9/12	Date 9/25	Date	Date	Date
Testina	SLDR	SLDR	SLDR	SLDR	SLDR
Kayla	SLDR	SLDR	SLDR	SLDR	SLDR
Chris	SLDR	SLDR	SLDR	SLDR	SLDR
Renaud	SLDR	SLDR	SLDR	SLDR	SLDR
Sheena	SLDR	SLDR	SLDR	SLDR	SLDR
Haroon	SLDR	SLDR	SLDR	SLDR	SLDR
Jonah	SLDR	SLDR	SLDR	SLDR	SLDR
Bambi	SLDR	SLDR	SLDR	SLDR	SLDR
Mackenzie	SLDR	SLDR	SLDR	SLDR	SLDR
Sandra	SLDR	SLDR	SLDR	SLDR	SLDR
Colin	SLDR	SLDR	SLDR	SLDR	SLDR
Cara	SLDR	SLDR	SLDR	SLDR	SLDR
Dakota	SLDR	SLDR	SLDR	SLDR	SLDR
Teran	SLDR	SLDR	SLDR	SLDR	SLDR

Figure 2-12

Acronyms to Support Specific Feedback and Recording Observations

Chemistry Lab Observations Acronym: **SCRAPP**	Decision-Making Process in Large- or Small-Group Settings (across disciplines) Acronym: **SMIER**
Safe work habits **C**onfidence **R**ecords as observes **A**ccurate and reliable **P**lan is followed **P**erseveres	**S**urveys options **M**akes decision **I**mplements decision **E**valuates implementation **R**eflects on process

Example 2 Conversations: *A high school world issues teacher created a three-point performance grid that identified what it would sound like if students were describing a concept at the highest level (proficient). Students would independently:*

- *use appropriate and accurate vocabulary*
- *make connections between the issue or event and other past or current issues or events*
- *include a thesis statement*
- *include several supporting details*
- *demonstrate logical thinking and reasoning*
- *describe the issue or event so that others outside the class could understand*
- *express ideas clearly and simply*
- *use analogies and metaphors*

From there she described students' abilities to do this at two other levels: beginning and expanding. She also shared the performance grid with students and then explained the nuances in quality differences among levels. As she listened to students in conversation with herself and others, she used the descriptors to determine where in the performance grid each student's level of competency lay. She used this performance grid throughout the entire semester because it related to a process rather than a specific product. She reviewed this data and identified what and how to teach in the following days and lessons.

Example 3 Products: *One large urban school district re-designed its grade book structure. Instead of teachers chronologically entering marks or scores, they made notes about content standards or outcomes. In the example from an English class shown in Figure 2-13, the outcomes are listed across the top of the grade book. Under each outcome, there are columns that allow assignments* related to that outcome to be recorded. Many assignments appear in more than one outcome; teachers can determine a student's level of achievement against the outcomes. Teachers can also see which outcomes have a breadth of evidence and which outcomes require more evidence in order to provide sufficient data over time and from multiple sources.

Figure 2-13

Grade Book Grouping by Outcomes/Standards

Students Type	Conv	Pro	Pro	Obs	Pro	Enhance Presentation Obs	Pro	Share Ideas and Information	Work in Groups
								Click on above to view marks related to this standard	
Testina	1	3	3	3	3	3	3		
Kayla	2.5		3			2	3		
Chris	2.5	3	3	3	3	3	3		
Renaud	2	2	3	3	2		2		
Sheena	3		2	3					
Haroon	2.5		3	3	3	3	3		
Jonah	3	2.5	3	3	3	3	3		
Bambi	3	abs	abs	2.5	3	3	2		
Mackenzie	3	1	3	3	3	3	2		
Sandra	2		2	3	2	2.5	2		
Colin	3	3	2		2	3	2		
Cara	3	2	3	3	3	3	3		
Dakota	1		2	3	3	3	3		
Teran	3		abs						
Harriet	3		3	3	3	3	3		
Dustyn	3	3	3	3	3		3		
Brennan	3	3	3	3	3	3	3		
Jordan	3	2	3	3	2	3	3		
Zachary	1		2.5	3	2	2	2		
Coltan	3		2.5	2	2	2	2		

*Conv=Conversations   Obs=Observations   Pro=Products

Teachers understand that their professional judgments of students' achievement are dependent on collecting evidence that is both reliable and valid. They deliberately plan to collect that evidence from observations, conversations, and products. They do not do this alone. Though teachers observe students both in process and in conversation and make notes that can be collated or considered, the student is also actively involved in the process of evidence collection. As learners self-assess and reflect, and as they create, write, and draw, they produce evidence that can be selected for placement in a portfolio or can be provided to the teacher for feedback, assessment, and evaluation. This is a joint process and does not rest solely with the teacher or the learner.

For example, in the social studies unit *Urban Spaces*, students not only produce all the products that have been listed (paragraphs describing rural, urban, and remote places; organizers to represent various urban, rural, and remote settlements; admit and exit slips; mind maps; article analyses; letters to community leadership; field notes; written responses to issues inherent in living in rural, urban, and remote places; graphs and maps; brochures; persuasive writing; research questions; electronic presentations; sort-and-predict frames and reports) but also make strategic selections from their work to provide evidence of their learning in portfolios. A social studies four-pocket portfolio might have the following sections, for example: demonstrates an understanding of the

▼ **Figure 2-14**

Photograph of Four-Pocket Portfolio

With thanks to Holly Tornrose of Bethel, ME.

concepts studied; communicates ideas with purpose and audience in mind; demonstrates active citizenship; and collaborates with others. (See Figure 2-14 for an example from English language arts.) It is the student who determines the work that best shows her competencies in these areas. Selection is an active process and, during the process of putting the portfolio together, students come to more deeply understand the work and their relation to it. Students' conversations with self (that is, self-assessment on ability to listen, express views and perspectives, and on journal entries that document the stages of work towards the end-of-semester project) might also be considered.

In the biology unit *Digestion and Nutrition*, the teacher observes the students at work and during the learning. The teacher also listens to the conversations that the students engage in, in both large- and small-group settings. However, if students clearly understand what is being observed and listened to, they can self- and peer assess – that is, they can collect the information in relation to criteria that have been shared or constructed together. So, for example, if students know what is expected of them during labs, they can reflect on their experience or what they observed in the work of their peers. They can then use a checklist or a met/not-yet-met frame to assess which lab criteria were present in their work that day and which criteria were not observed. This information is helpful to the student as he works towards meeting the criteria; areas of focus for future labs have now been identified.

Here are five examples of how some teachers make it possible for students to collect evidence from a variety of sources – products, conversations, and observations:

> **Example 1:** *A teacher of a career options course has his students place evidence in their binders in these areas:*
> - *working as a team member*
> - *solving problems*
> - *communicating clearly*
>
> **Example 2:** *A high school fashion technology teacher has students take pictures of the clothing that they have created over the semester. Students include pictures of each step in the process, along with a few statements that describe what they learned in each phase:*
> - *creative inspiration*
> - *getting ready to work with fabric*

- *sewing an article of clothing*
- *accessorizing clothing*

Example 3: *A band teacher has students collect audio recordings of music from various genres. Each student creates an MP3 file with a minimum of four pieces that demonstrate his versatility as a musician. Students pair the recording with prompts for each piece that begin with this statement, "As you listen to this piece of music, please notice . . . "*

Example 4: *A high school mathematics teacher used two two-pocket portfolios (taped together) and labelled each pocket with a concept or big idea from the course. Students looked through their notebooks and other places where they collected work and selected samples from products, conversations, and observations to provide evidence of their learning. The teacher identified four categories:*

- *demonstrates persistence in mathematics*
- *accurately uses mathematical language*
- *connects mathematics to self, others, and the real world*
- *applies mathematical concepts to problem-solving situations*

Example 5: *A social studies teacher collected daily work samples, projects, and test results. She also asked students to collect evidence from class work about key social studies skills that she identified as essential to being a social scientist. She explained that during every class there would be times when they would be expected to engage as a social scientist. She would collect observations and the students would collect evidence. After analyzing the social studies content standards, she defined the term social scientist and had each student keep a four-pocket portfolio like the following:*

- *Pocket 1: Proficient Writer*
- *Pocket 2: Productive Researcher*
- *Pocket 3: Collaborative Group Worker*
- *Pocket 4: Student-Selected Goal*

Students kept track of evidence and were asked to reflect regularly on how they were improving as social scientists.

Social media have expanded the possibilities for extending our community by changing the way we communicate and stay in touch. Communication can still be print-based, but, more and more often, the possibilities include such methods as emails; class or student blogs; interaction in online communities; twitter tweets; work samples (digital or analogue); presentations (in person or online, in school or at home); and files and portfolios (digital or analogue) containing collections of evidence. In order to use social media in building community and supporting students to communicate their learning to others (not just parents), it is important that they connect it to the learning they do.

Teachers are reminded that every subject area has a communication thread that is unique to the discipline. Communicating with others in ways appropriate to the discipline not only gives students practice (while also giving teachers evidence), but provides an audience for the communication. Secondly, since the people doing the work are learning the most, it is the students who need to be doing most of the communicating.

Here are some examples that highlight ways that students are communicating what they are learning.

- *In the last couple of minutes of each class, a high school English teacher asks a small group of students to compose a brief email outlining what was learned that day. The message is sent to the students' parents through a distribution list. When parents receive the email, they can reply to the teacher and/or their children.*

- *In a history class, students create their own blogs. On a regular basis, students post to their blogs a narrative of what they are learning in the class; they attach digital documents and images of their class work. Students also add self-assessments. These self-assessments constitute a digital recording of students' reflections on the work that they have been doing. For example, they talk about improvements that they have noticed in their work in relation to the criteria that had been set. Parents have password access to the blogs, as does the teacher. The blog and its required parts are a significant product (that includes conversation) that is considered in the final grade for the class.*

- *In a science class, the teacher posts the curriculum standards to the classroom website and the student-friendly version of the learning destination. At the end of each quarter, students electronically attach the best evidence of learning that they have from their work showing what they have met or are working towards. They make this available to their teacher and parents.*

- *In a high school integrated program (English, social studies, science and technology), students create an electronic portfolio each term. The focus of the portfolio is not around a single standard of the program for that particular term but, rather, on student-selected evidence that adds to the evidence the teacher has collected via the end-of-unit culminating activities. So, for example, if a student has struggled with comprehension and literary analysis all term, she might include in her portfolio another essay that could demonstrate her attainment of that learning. The portfolio is submitted to the teacher to use as evidence in determining the term grade. It is also available for parents to view online. Parents get a good sense of the areas in which their children have struggled and the ways in which they have worked to prove that they have addressed their learning gaps.*

In summary, as teachers ask students to provide evidence of learning in the ways described above, they go farther and have students select the proof of learning in relation to the standards-based learning goals for the course (the student-friendly learning destination shared with students early in the course). Because the teacher has planned for a variety of triangulated evidence, this process helps students come to understand that success has many different looks; evidence of what one has learned can be shown in a variety of ways. Students also come to understand that they have a responsibility to show proof of learning. Teachers also need to collect evidence of student learning and they must help students to become involved in communicating that learning to others. Teachers know that they are successful when their learners are engaged and motivated *and* know how to *give* help, how to *get* help, *what* help to get, and *how* to use the help to improve their learning.

Now that students are engaged, motivated, learning, collecting evidence of learning alongside teachers, and communicating their learning to others, it is time for teachers to plan the summative assessment: the evaluation process. In the next section – After the Learning – we will help you do just that in four easy steps:

1. finalizing the collection of evidence of learning (including the role of formative and summative assessment evidence)
2. making informed professional judgments
3. reporting learning and achievement using required format (percentages, letter grades, number grades, or other symbols)
4. involving students in the reporting process

After the Learning: Evaluating and Reporting to Others

CHAPTER 3

CONTENTS

Finalizing the Collection of Evidence of Learning

Making Informed Professional Judgments

Reporting Learning and Achievement Using Required Format

Involving Students in the Reporting Process

"Summative assessment by teachers is the process by which teachers gather evidence in a planned and systematic way in order to draw inferences about their students' learning, based on their professional judgment, and to report at a particular time on their students' achievements."

Assessment Reform Group (2006, p. 4)

"Evaluation and reporting occur at the point in the classroom assessment cycle when the learning pauses, and the evidence is organized and evaluated by comparing it to what students needed to learn. Then, the results of the evaluation are shared through the reporting process" (Davies, 2011, p. 93). As teachers approach reporting time having begun with the end in mind, having thought through evidence of learning, and having involved students in the assessment process and in collecting evidence of learning, stress is significantly diminished. The hard work of teaching and learning is almost done. The evidence collections are complete. Students have shared their perspectives on what they have learned. Teachers are now ready to make their professional judgments and then report.

As they do these last tasks, teachers review the evidence that they have collected. Some teachers choose to compile and collate it. Others do not. What all teachers do is make decisions about which evidence best shows what students now know and understand and can do and articulate in relation to those standards and expectations that have guided the teaching and learning.

> **What About...?**
>
> What about the students who don't do anything in class throughout the term or semester and then, at the end, hand most of their work in and show up to take the final exam? They pass based on work that is done at the last moment. It's not right.
>
> We need to take a look at our definition of success in our classes and how we communicate that to students. For some students, if tests and assignments are all that matters, there is no reason to participate in class. Re-defining what matters and what counts is important in this instance.
>
> (To read more about this, see What About 3-1? on page 84.)

Once the evidence of learning has been reviewed, teachers compare that evidence to the level of quality that was expected and make informed professional judgments through ongoing work with colleagues. Then, teachers use this professional judgment to communicate in the report card, using the required symbols and narrative comments. Lastly, teachers arrange to have students show evidence of their learning to parents either at home, at school, or online, and invite parents to meet with them if they have additional questions. That's it! Done! And done well!

Now, let's review this process step-by-step so you can make your own plans. *After* the learning, and as you move on to evaluating and reporting, there are four tasks:

1. finalizing the collection of evidence of learning (including the role of formative and summative evidence)
2. making informed professional judgments
3. reporting learning and achievement using required format (percentages, letter grades, number grades, or other symbols)
4. involving students in the reporting process

1. Finalizing the Collection of Evidence of Learning

After the learning, students and teachers revisit, for the last time, their collections of evidence in relation to the student-friendly learning destination. Teachers ask students to look for the best proof that they have met *all* the learning standards or outcomes for the course. Since everything that a student says, does, or creates is potentially evidence, this is the time when students make the best case for what they have learned. When students have determined their best evidence in relation to the learning destination, they present the collection to their teacher, along with an explanation about why they think it is proof of learning – that is, of reaching or reaching towards the standard/outcome/expectation that was their goal.

Teachers review the evidence of learning that students have collected and the evidence that they themselves have collected over time. This includes observations, conversations, and products, which may be in numeric or qualitative form. As teachers examine the evidence, they consider "best evidence" in terms of validity and reliability. This standards-based grading and reporting process honours teachers' informed professional judgment and provides a way for teachers to support students as they take a variety of learning pathways to success and quality. It is both fair and equitable.

Now that there is a collection of evidence to represent the students' learning, it is time for teachers to make an informed professional judgment.

2. Making Informed Professional Judgments

Evaluating and reporting are less stressful and can be done with confidence when they are the last steps in a purposeful, systematic, multi-step process that does not come into play just at the end of learning. Rather, it begins when teachers come to understand the standards or learning outcomes and the appropriate quality levels expected for a particular course or grade level. Evaluating and reporting are further informed when teachers meet with others to come to a common understanding of quality and expectations. Then, once the evidence of learning has been collected from multiple sources over time, teachers begin a process of examining the evidence – both qualitative and quantitative – and making a decision regarding whether and to what degree students know, understand, can apply, and can articulate what is detailed by the standards or learning outcomes.

Evaluating and reporting require professional judgment in the context of the following four questions:

1. What does the student know, what is she or he able to do, and what can she or he articulate?
2. What areas require further attention or development?
3. In what ways can the student's learning be supported?
4. How is the student progressing in relation to the expectations for students in a similar age range?

Making a professional judgment is a purposeful, systematic, multi-step process. This process does not come into play just at the end of learning. Professional judgment becomes more informed with reflection, practice, and ongoing collegial conversations that involve looking at student work from classrooms that are using protocols and examining student data generated from a variety of sources. (See Figure 3-1.) The protocol that colleagues used at an earlier stage to come to a common understanding of quality can be used again during and after the learning to check and affirm that the earlier views of quality are still commonly held.

▼ **Figure 3-1**

Reaching Agreement about Quality

1. Appoint a timekeeper and facilitator. Begin.
2. The presenting teacher describes the evidence. (2 minutes)
3. Three reviewers ask questions to clarify. (3 minutes)
4. Group members review the work. They discuss the work in relation to excellence (e.g., A) while the presenting teacher listens. (5-7 minutes)
5. The presenting teacher joins the conversation and points out anything that might have been missed. (2 minutes)
6. Each participant sums up by commenting on where they think the evidence is in relation to excellence. (5 minutes)
7. The presenting teacher reflects on the process. The group reflects on the process. (5 minutes)
8. Repeat the process with another teacher providing another body of evidence for one student.

© Copyright – Classroom Connections International Inc. www.connect2learning.com

As we have said numerous times in this text and deliberately repeat now, *everything* a student says, does, or creates is potentially evidence of learning. It is important that teachers use the evidence available for each student and compare it to the standards or learning outcomes that students are expected to learn. In a standards-based evaluation system, teachers have to account for each student's learning in relation to the expectations for that grade and subject area and, we stress, not compare his or her work to the work of other students in the class.

As mentioned earlier, informed professional judgment results from teaching to the standards or learning outcomes based on a common reporting scale (often decided by the jurisdiction); it is also based on thoughtfully considering samples of student work and collections of evidence, scoring common assessments, and analyzing external test data with colleagues. While a teacher's written and verbal comments may speak to the amount of *growth* students have made in their learning, the evaluation must reflect their progress in relation to the standards for the subject area or course and the grade level at which they are working.

While teachers do not have to base their evaluation decision on the same body of evidence of learning for each student, they must base their evaluation on a reliable and valid collection of evidence of learning. And this evaluation must be equitable – that is, all students, regardless of how they learn, show their learning, or how much they struggle (or not), must have the same opportunities to show proof of learning. A helpful definition of the term *informed professional judgment* is: the professional determination, after a review of evidence of learning present (not absent), of what has been learned and achieved.

We need to stress that adding the scores and averaging them misrepresents the learning that has been accomplished. To evaluate well, we should look at *all* the evidence: observations, products, and conversations. *Triangulation of evidence* is essential because it puts single pieces of evidence into context. Just as a judge in a court of law must examine all the evidence in light of the legal statutes, teachers must look at all the evidence in light of the description of learning based on the standards or learning outcomes. They must consider the entire range of information (all the quantitative and qualitative data): the evidence students have collected, the self-assessments they have made, their observations, criteria-based assessments attached to projects or assignments, and the evidence that teachers have collected, including performance grids, rubric scores, and grades from projects and tests. As teachers examine all the evidence, they are seeking to make the most informed and defensible final professional judgment possible.

It is at this point that many of the "hot issues" currently being debated about reporting cease to matter. For example, whether the evidence of learning was produced in the midst of learning time (formative) or at the end of learning time (summative) isn't an issue. The timing is just information for the teacher. The Assessment Reform Group (2006, p. 10) states: "For summative purposes, common criteria need to be applied and achievement is summarized in terms of levels or grades, which must have the same meaning for all pupils. This means that if the information already gathered and used formatively is to be used for summative assessment it must be reviewed against the broader criteria that define reporting levels or grades. Change over time can be taken into account so that preference is given to the best evidence that shows the pupil's achievement across a range of work during the period covered by the summative assessment." Further, if that evidence was turned in late, or never submitted and received a zero mark, or if it was submitted after six feedback cycles with the teacher, it is, once again, simply information about the evidence itself.

What About…?

What do I do with students who turn in their work late, or maybe not at all?

If our default stance is to deduct marks or assign a score of zero, students quickly realize that there is nothing in it for them to turn in their work. What other consequences can be put in place and what other supports can be identified so that the natural response to not turning work in is not to abandon it but rather to get it done?

(To read more about this, see What About 3-2? on page 85.)

In summary, we state emphatically that what matters is that the final evaluation *must* represent students' actual learning and achievement in relation to the standards or learning outcomes for the course. Many jurisdictions have clearly identified guidelines to support and clearly communicate the principles that serve as a foundation to the act of reporting. (See Figure 3-2, which is adapted from *Transforming Schools and Systems Using Assessment: A Practical Guide* (2012) by Davies, Herbst & Parrott Reynolds).

Figure 3-2

> **Reporting Guidelines – Checking for Alignment and Consistency**
>
> **Agreement about Quality**
>
> The Learning Destination (in relation to Standards or Outcomes)
>
> 1. Are report card grades given for the full range of educational standards or outcomes, not just those easiest to measure?
> 2. Has evidence of learning been selected because of its alignment with outcomes and standards?
>
> Reliable and Valid Evidence of Learning
>
> 3. Are the report card grades based upon a wide array of evidence from multiple sources over time so as to ensure validity and reliability?
> 4. Do students understand expectations and acceptable evidence?
> 5. Are students involved in co-constructing criteria in relation to products, processes, and collections of evidence of learning?
> 6. Does your summative evaluation take place after students have time and opportunity to learn?
>
> Evaluation at the End of Learning in Preparation for Reporting
>
> 7. Are your report card grades derived from evidence present, not absent (thus devoid of practices such as assigning zeros or penalty deductions as a default stance, grading on a curve, averaging)?
> 8. Are report card grades for achievement of standards or learning outcomes reported separately from other non-achievement factors such as effort, attitude, attendance, and punctuality?
> 9. Are the report card grades reflective of a student's most consistent, more recent pattern of performance in relation to course learning goals based on the relevant standards and outcomes, as well as pre-determined levels of quality?
>
> Informed Professional Judgment
>
> 10. Do the report card grades reflect informed teacher professional judgment of the level of quality of student work in relation to the standards or outcomes?
> 11. Are report card grades validated by and anchored in collaborative conversation and analysis of student work against agreed-upon criteria by teachers across grade levels and subjects?
> 12. Are report card grades reflective of and illustrated by collections of exemplars and samples that illustrate levels of quality and achievement?
>
> © 2012 Davies, Herbst, and Parrott Reynolds. *Transforming Schools and Systems Using Assessment: A Practical Guide*. (pp. 103-104).

3. Reporting Learning and Achievement Using Required Format

Once teachers have exercised their professional judgment, and once that final judgment has been made, they represent their decision using a percentage, letter grade, number grade, symbol, comment, or narrative – whatever form is required by policy and regulation. In order to finalize the report, teachers summarize students' strengths and areas needing improvement, and students and parents review the evidence. We use the term *reporting process* because reporting is not merely an event that produces a product – that is, the report card – but rather, it is a process that includes the work before teachers meet with students, during the learning time, and at the end.

The following two examples are accounts from teachers who were required to report using percentage grades. As you read, reflect on what you can learn from them. Consider what is similar to your own reporting process and what is different. Ask yourself, "Is there anything in this account that can help improve my reporting process?"

Example 1: *Melissa Labbe teaches high school mathematics and is required to report using percentages. The standards detail both the concepts and mathematical processes that students are to learn. Melissa collects evidence of student learning in relation to the key concepts. The evidence consists of assignments, quizzes, and tests. Melissa asks students to also collect evidence of their learning during the term. She challenges them to show proof of learning in relation to mathematic processes such as perseverance, questioning, drawing on past knowledge and experience, and precision of language and thought. She calls them mathematical "habits of mind" (Costa & Kallick, 2000). The evidence that each student selects in each category is put in simple, inexpensive four-pocket portfolios where each pocket is labelled. Students are given brief chunks of time during the term to select the best evidence they have in relation to the "habits of mind" categories for the course. They might draw evidence from their in-class work, home practice work, tests, quizzes, or some work produced for another subject or course that they have put in their portfolios. This portfolio is designed so that students can show that they are improving. Then, they take time to explain in writing why a particular piece of evidence shows proof of improvement in that area. At the end of the learning time, they make their final selections and reflections and submit their portfolios. Melissa then uses a rubric she co-constructed with students and makes her professional judgment – that is, she evaluates the work. The resulting evaluation is 20 percent of the final grade. The remaining 80 percent of the students' report card grade is based on the most recent, most consistent evidence of learning in relation to the major concepts taught in the term (Labbe, 2013).*

Example 2: *Mr. W is required to report using percentages. He has defined what it means to be a successful student in Biology 11 and shared this with students and parents. Mr. W collects evidence of learning and students collect evidence of learning. At the end of the term, Mr. W based 40 percent of the* *final grade on evidence collected in relation to the definition of quality titled "Being a Scientist." During the term, students collect the best evidence they have that they are "being a scientist" and then, towards the end of the term, make their final selections. They select two or three pieces of work in each of the five categories in "Being a Scientist" and put it in a folder. (See Figure 3-3.) The remaining 60 percent of their grade is based on scores, observations, and interview notes that Mr. W has collected over the term from projects, tests, and exams.*

Figure 3-3 ▼

Being a Scientist in Biology 11

Learning Destination	Evidence of Learning might include:	My Evidence of Learning: (Students, please note what evidence you are submitting.)	As you review this evidence of learning in Biology 11, please notice that… (Students, please explain why it is important evidence of learning.)
1. I understand and apply the scientific concepts being studied. 2. I understand and apply the scientific processes being studied. 3. I ask and answer questions about the world. 4. I articulate clear understandings of the scientific process. 5. I make connections to other concepts, to other situations, and to life.	• graphic organizers • lab reports • presentations • notes from group work • experiment demonstrations • self- and peer assessments • reading summaries and reflections • video sequences • research projects • tests, quizzes, tasks		
Other? If you have additional thoughts or ideas about what is important when being a scientist, add them here. This is your opportunity to include evidence of learning that I might have not considered.			

In the following three examples, teachers are required to report using letters, terms, or number grades. In each account, the teacher has decided to expand the description of a letter or number grade beyond a numerical range so that it also includes the quality of the evidence that is expected. In this way, the letter or number grade better aligns the reporting practice with the standards or learning outcomes upon which they are responsible for reporting. As you read, consider what you can learn from these three accounts. Reflect on what is similar to your reporting process and what is different. Ask yourself, "Is there anything in these accounts that can help us improve our reporting process?"

Example 1: *In a school that has elected to move towards using level descriptors, high school teacher David Mindorff prepares for reporting student learning in his International Baccalaureate (IB) theory of knowledge class by comparing written descriptions of what a high-quality performance would look like for each standard against actual student work. (See Figure 3-4.)*

▼ **Figure 3-4**

Distinguished Achievement in IB Theory of Knowledge

- demonstrates a comprehensive understanding of the strengths and limitations of the various *Ways of Knowing* and of the methods used in the different *Areas of Knowledge*
- consistently demonstrates a comprehensive understanding that personal views, judgments, and beliefs may influence their own knowledge claims and those of others
- demonstrates an exceptional capacity to reason and reflect critically, showing insight
- consistently identifies the values underlying judgment and knowledge claims, pertinent to local and global issues
- consistently demonstrates a balanced approach to inquiry by evaluating claims and counterclaims
- uses concise and precise oral and written language to formulate and communicate ideas clearly
- displays exceptionally supportive seminar behaviour including consistently referencing the ideas of others, consistently encouraging the participation of others, and constantly listening and contributing to discussions
- writing is structured excellently with a logically coherent development leading to an effective conclusion
- journal exceeds standards for all aspects
- consistently makes highly effective connections between and across a wide variety of *Ways of Knowing* and *Areas of Knowledge*
- consistently makes effective connections between personal experience and different *Ways of Knowing* and *Areas of Knowledge* (journal)
- consistently demonstrates a comprehensive understanding of knowledge at work in the world

© 2013 Davies, Herbst, and Busick (Eds.) *Quality Assessment in High Schools: Accounts From Teachers* (Mindorff, p. 164).

Example 2: *A high school biology teacher examined all the required outcomes and divided them into two categories: scientific method and scientific concepts. Since he was on a yearly schedule with four terms and four report cards, he chunked the concepts into eight units of study–two for each term. He then detailed what was important for students to know, do, and be able to articulate about scientific inquiry and included that description as part of each unit of study. As he planned, he identified the products, performance tasks, assignments, quizzes, and tests that he wanted to collect. He also summarized the description of scientific inquiry and created three categories: beginning, on-the-way, and proficient. He described what he would see, hear, and have as physical evidence if students were engaged in scientific inquiry during in-class processing times. This became his observation guide. Then he made a student-friendly version, which he shared with students, explaining that they would need to collect and submit evidence along with a reflection at the end of each unit of study. He suggested that they keep the evidence in a digital notebook and encouraged them to record their reflections. As the year progressed, the students received grades based on the collections of evidence of learning that they gathered and what the teacher collected in relation to the learning outcomes. Students had multiple opportunities to show proof of learning within each unit. They also had multiple opportunities across all the units to show how they were improving in terms of scientific method. Their final grades were based on their most recent evidence of learning in terms of scientific method and the final grades for each content unit.*

Example 3: *A team of Grade 9 mathematics teachers met at the beginning of the school year and developed a description of success for Grade 9 mathematics. They deliberately included both qualitative and quantitative data because they were committed to collecting evidence from multiple sources so all standards could be evaluated. They included the results of school-wide assessments, as well as the common assessment upon which their grade level had agreed. Each teacher also collected a range of evidence based on classroom work. This work had been designed to support each individual learner, and so it varied from student to student and class to class. In order to evaluate and to be clear to students and parents about how student learning in mathematics would be evaluated, the teachers developed criteria that* described success (see Figure 3-5 below). *They also took time in their weekly planning sessions to review student work and, over the course of a semester, created a collection of samples (based on student work) that represented the quality expected of "A"-level work. Each teacher received a set of samples to use with students and parents. In addition, since each class had groups of students working at different levels, they researched developmental continua in the area of mathematics, problem-solving, and numeracy and began an inquiry project focused on mathematics development so they could evaluate with more confidence.*

▼ **Figure 3-5**

Mathematics—Defining an "A"

Evidence of learning collected over time from multiple sources demonstrates student learning by consistently and independently producing proof of learning.

Student consistently and independently...

- understands, remembers, and applies mathematical concepts being studied
- articulates clear understanding of mathematical concepts and is able to give everyday examples of use
- applies concepts, skills, and strategies to problems
- analyzes problems, uses a variety of effective strategies to find possible solutions, and is able to check and evaluate the effectiveness of the process used
- works effectively by self and with others
- communicates effectively using words, symbols, and representations
- connects ideas to self, to others, and to other ideas or tasks
- uses mathematical 'habits of mind' including, for example, persistence, questioning, drawing on past knowledge, and precision of language and thought

Proof of learning includes work collected over time:

- products (e.g., work samples, tests, quizzes)
- observations (e.g., class work, demonstrations, performance tasks, teacher observations)
- conversations (e.g., discussions, written reflections, journal entries, conferences, interviews)

Numerical Data:

- common assessment scores: (typically receive rubric scores of 4 and 5 on a five-point scale)
- summative evaluations (e.g., performance tasks, projects, tests, and quizzes receive grades in the 91% - 100% range)

When we evaluate, we determine the worth, or value, of the evidence; we appraise it with respect to excellence, or merit. Simply totalling the marks or grades in our record books means that important evidence may not be considered, and the learning will therefore not be accurately represented. When evaluating, teachers must be especially careful as they work with numbers from performance scales and rubrics. Totalling scores from rubrics and averaging them with other kinds of numbers is like adding mangoes, potatoes, apples, and trees. It does not make mathematical sense. After all, a great score on a quiz that focuses on simple mathematical operations is not equal to, and should not be weighted the same as, work that involves the kind of complex problem-solving that contains multiple operations and explanations of the choices made along the way.

> ### What About...?
>
> *Some parents don't value educators' professional judgment. Some even challenge what we record on a report card.*
>
> Some parents ask questions that seem to question our professionalism. We respond in a thoughtful and reasoned manner. The curriculum standards, samples, criteria, and the voices of their children can assist as we engage parents in important conversations.
>
> *(To read more about this, see What About 3-3? on page 87.)*

After the report card has been prepared, it is time to involve students in communicating with others about their learning.

4. Involving Students in the Reporting Process

Formal evaluating and reporting is usually required by legislation or policy and is a process of looking at the evidence, having conversations and conferences about what the evidence means, and keeping a written record of the evaluation for each learner's permanent file. Reporting used to be an event that happened only at set times in a year. Now, in many jurisdictions, examining and making sense of a student's learning is becoming an ongoing process that involves students, parents, and teachers.

It is not only teachers who have the responsibility for evaluating and reporting. Students and parents, too, have a role in evaluating and reporting. Students do the learning and create evidence of learning along the way. In preparation for evaluation and reporting, students organize their evidence of learning and summarize their strengths, needs, and plans for more learning. They present the evidence to account for their learning to others and receive feedback. Then they set goals for future learning. Parents, legal guardians, or other adults selected by the student participate by looking at the evidence, by listening, watching, asking questions, and making sense of the evidence in relation to the standards. They interpret the evidence and the accompanying self-assessments that students present; they also interpret the commentary given by the teacher.

When students and their parents are engaged in reviewing the evidence and affirming whether or not the evaluation makes sense, sound professional judgments by teachers are more likely to have been made, simply because information has been provided by others. Every time students speak with their parents about learning, they are reporting. That is, whenever students take home a sample of their work and discuss it or invite parents to a portfolio afternoon to look at their work, they are reporting to parents about their learning. Increasingly, teachers are involving secondary students in the conferencing and reporting process and inviting them and their parents to be part of student-parent-teacher conferences. The purpose of these conferences is to look at the evidence, highlight strengths, consider and discuss areas needing improvement, and set goals during the reporting period.

Lynn Sueoka, who teaches freshmen and sophomores in a media communications and technology learning centre in an urban high school, uses digital portfolios as a communication tool to expand the circle of learning to include parents and others. She requires students to post an online portfolio of their evidence of learning in relation to the standards. She explains to students that it is important for them to use evidence that has not yet been evaluated as part of their program. Students share their portfolios with their parents or guardians outside of class time. Many choose to share it with others as well. This structure allows for families to interact at a time and in a place that suits them best. For example, parents who work shifts can access the portfolio late in an evening, and families whose first language is not the language of instruction can engage in conversations about the learning. As Lynn reflects in "A Culture of Learning: Building a Community of Shared Learning Through Student Online Portfolios," this process is ". . . so different from the point rationing and number crunching of my earlier years in teaching" (Sueoka, 2013, p. 154).

Gregory et al. (2011) detail a step-by-step process for a student-teacher conference that allows students to present their learning to teachers in preparation for evaluation. The materials presented for these conferences can be used later for a student-parent conference.

As we stated earlier, teachers' professional lives might be simpler if evaluating and reporting could be tidy and "objective." However, the process of making evaluations informed by a teacher's professional judgment is inherently subjective. The more reliable and valid the evidence collected and the longer the period of time over which it is collected, the more confidence everyone can have in the professional judgment that has been made. By looking for patterns and trends over time, based on multiple sources (triangulation) of reliable and valid evidence, teachers can report with confidence.

As we focus on summative, end-of-term grading and reporting, it is important that we revisit the evidence that was collected during the learning - evidence that was formative in nature. It is critical that classroom teachers review all the evidence of learning collected over time in order to make an informed professional judgment. The Assessment Reform Group put it this way:

> Innumerable classroom events enable teachers to gather information about pupils by observing, questioning, listening to informal discussions and reviewing written work. In formative assessment this information may be used immediately to help pupils or it may be stored and used to plan future learning opportunities...
>
> For formative assessment the evidence is interpreted in relation to the progress of a pupil towards the goals of a particular section of work. Next steps are decided according to what has been achieved and what problems have been encountered. The interpretation is in terms of *what to do to help further learning*, not what level or grade a pupil has reached (ARG, 2006, pp. 9, 10).

Teachers assist students in collecting and showing proof of their learning. They support students as they communicate their learning with parents. Teachers make themselves available to discuss how they have evaluated the students' work and to discuss with parents the ways that their students' learning could be better supported. In the end, teachers are the final arbitrators and evaluators of their students' work. It is their professional responsibility.

Now that you have exercised your professional judgment and have reported on your students' achievements, it is important to reflect on the entire process and take time to research, refine, and revise . . . and start again.

Afterword: Until the Next Time

"If you want to build a ship, don't drum up people together to collect wood and don't assign them tasks and work, but rather teach them to long for the endless immensity of the sea.

Quand tu veux construire un bateau, ne commence pas par rassembler du bois, couper des planches et distribuer du travail, mais reveille au sein des hommes le desir de la mer grande et large."

Antoine de Saint-Exupéry

We began by stating that we would demonstrate the "simplicity that lies beyond complexity." We believe that these ideas are just that – simple ideas that work for the complex task of classroom assessment, evaluation, and reporting. That said, classroom assessment is complicated by the context: the students with whom we work, our colleagues, time constraints, regulations and policies, outside mandates, and more. As professionals, we are always doing the best we can given what we know, so it is important that we continue to learn and be informed.

Between now and the next time you engage in classroom assessment and standards-based reporting, consider:

- reflecting on what is working, what is not, and possible next steps towards continued improvement
- researching more about classroom assessment, evaluation, and reporting
- conducting an inquiry into your classroom assessment, evaluation, and reporting practices
- writing your own narrative to deepen your understanding and better prepare you to support the growing understanding of others
- working with colleagues to build shared understanding of quality and success in relation to standards or learning outcomes

As you learn more and inform your professional judgment through reflection, research, and ongoing collegial conversations, your students will benefit. And, in the end, that is what matters. After all, none of us are in education for the "big bucks;" we are in education to make a difference. And, research from around the world (Norway, 2011) clearly documents the idea that classroom assessment has the greatest effect on learning and achievement of any education innovation ever documented.

It is as simple, and as complex, as that.

> *"The art of simplicity is a puzzle of complexity."*
> *Doug Horton*

References

Assessment Reform Group (ARG). 2002. *Assessment for learning: 10 principles.* Pamphlet on research-based principles to guide classroom practice.

Assessment Reform Group (ARG). 2006. *The role of teachers in the assessment of learning.* Pamphlet produced by Assessment Systems for the Future project (ASF). http://arrts.gtcni.org.uk/gtcni/handle/2428/4617

Berliner, D. and Biddle, B. 1998. *The Manufactured Crisis: Myths, Frauds and the Attack on America's Public Schools.* New York: Longman.

Black, P. and Wiliam, D. 1998. Inside the black box: Raising standards through classroom assessment. *Phi Delta Kappan* 80, no. 2: 1-20.

Black, P. and Wiliam, D. 2003. In praise of educational research: Formative assessment. *British Educational Research Journal* 29, no. 5: 623-637.

Black, P., Harrison, C., Lee, C., Marshall, B., and Wiliam, D. 2003. *Assessment for Learning: Putting it into Practice.* Berkshire, UK: Open University Press.

Burger, J., Perry, B., and Eagle, M. 2009. "Aggregating and analyzing classroom achievement data supplemental to external tests." In T.J. Kowalski and T.J. Lasley II (Eds.) *Handbook of Data-Based Decision Making in Education* pp. 317-343. New York: Routledge.

Butler, R. 1988. Enhancing and undermining intrinsic motivation: the effects of task-involving and ego-involving evaluation on interest. *British Journal of Educational Psychology* 58: 1-14.

Costa, A. and Kallick, B. 2000. *Assessing and Reporting on Habits of Mind.* Alexandria, VA: ASCD.

Covey, S. 2004. *The 7 Habits of Highly Effective People: Powerful Lessons in Personal Change.* New York: Simon & Schuster. https://www.stephencovey.com/7habits/7habits-habit2.php

Covington, M.V. 1998. *The Will to Learn: A Guide for Motivating Young People*. Cambridge, UK: Cambridge University Press.

Crooks, T. 1988. The impact of classroom evaluation practices on students. *Review of Educational Research* 58, no. 4: 438-481.

Darling-Hammond, L. and Richardson, N. February 2009. Teacher learning: What matters? *Educational Leadership* 66, no. 5: 46-53.

Davies, A. 2004. *Facilitator's Guide to Classroom Assessment K-12*. (Multimedia resource). Courtenay, BC: Connections Publishing.

Davies, A. 2008. *Assessment of Learning: A Professional Learning Resource on Standards-Based Grading and Reporting*. (Multimedia resource). Courtenay, BC: Connections Publishing.

Davies, A. 2010. *Assessment* for *Learning K-12*. (Multimedia resource). William Grindell video clip. Courtenay, BC: Connections Publishing.

Davies, A. 2011. *Making Classroom Assessment Work*, 3rd Edition. Courtenay, BC: Connections Publishing and Bloomington, IN: Solution Tree Press.

Davies, A., Herbst, S. and Busick, K. (Eds.). 2013. *Quality Assessment in High School: Accounts from Teachers*. Courtenay, BC: Connections Publishing and Bloomington, IN: Solution Tree Press.

Davies, A., Herbst, S., and Parrott Reynolds, B. 2012. *Transforming Schools and Systems Using Assessment: A Practical Guide*. Courtenay, BC: Connections Publishing and Bloomington, IN: Solution Tree Press.

Deci, E. and Ryan, R. M. 2002. *Handbook of Self-Determination Research*. New York: University of Rochester Press.

Dufour, R., Dufour, R., Eaker, R., and Many, T. 2006. *Learning By Doing: A Handbook for Professional Learning Communities at Work*. Bloomington, IN: Solution Tree Press.

Glaude, C. 2005. *Protocols for Professional Learning Conversations*. Courtenay, BC: Connections Publishing and Bloomington, IN: Solution Tree Press.

Glaude, C. 2010. *When Students Fail to Learn: Protocols for a School-Wide Response.* Courtenay, BC: Connections Publishing and Bloomington, IN: Solution Tree Press.

Gordon, S. and Reese, M. 1997. High stakes testing: Worth the price? *Journal of School Leadership* 7, no. 4: 345-368.

Gregory, K., Cameron, C., and Davies, A. 2011. *Setting and Using Criteria,* 2nd Edition. Courtenay, BC: Connections Publishing and Bloomington, IN: Solution Tree Press.

Gregory, K., Cameron, C., and Davies, A. 2011. *Self-Assessment and Goal Setting,* 2nd Edition. Courtenay, BC: Connections Publishing and Bloomington, IN: Solution Tree Press.

Gregory, K., Cameron, C., and Davies, A. 2011. *Conferencing and Reporting,* 2nd Edition. Courtenay, BC: Connections Publishing and Bloomington, IN: Solution Tree Press.

Guest, M. 2013. "Mathematics teachers are ahead of the curve when it comes to assessment *for* learning." In A. Davies, S. Herbst, and K. Busick. (Eds.), *Quality Assessment in High Schools: Accounts from Teachers* (pp. 103-107). Courtenay, BC: Connections Publishing and Bloomington, IN: Solution Tree Press.

Harlen, W. and Deakin Crick, R. 2002. *Testing, Motivation, and Learning.* Pamphlet produced by Assessment Reform Group at University of Cambridge Faculty of Education.

Harlen, W. and Deakin Crick, R. 2002. A systematic review of the impact of summative assessment and tests on students' motivation for learning (EPPI-Centre Review, version 1.1*) In: *Research Evidence in Education Library.* London; EPPI-Centre, Social Science Research Unit, Institute of Education.

Labbe, M. 2013. "Reflective assessment in mathematics." In A. Davies, S. Herbst, and K. Busick (Eds.), *Quality Assessment in High Schools: Accounts From Teachers* (pp. 131-135). Courtenay, BC: Connections Publishing and Bloomington, IN: Solution Tree Press.

Lincoln, Y. and Guba, E. 1984. *Naturalistic Inquiry*. Beverly Hills, CA: SAGE.

Looney, J. 2005. *Formative Assessment – Improving Learning in Secondary Classrooms*. London, UK: OECD Publishing.

Meisels, S., Atkins-Burnett, S., Xue, Y., Bickel, D.D., and Son, S.H. 2003. Creating a system of accountability: The impact of instructional assessment on elementary children's achievement scores. *Educational Policy Analysis Archives* 11, no. 9. 19 pages. Retrieved September 19, 2004 from http://epaa.asu.edu/ojs/article/view/237/363

Mindorff, D. 2013. "Assessment case studies: IB theory of knowledge and biology." In A. Davies, S. Herbst, and K. Busick (Eds.), *Quality Assessment in High Schools: Accounts From Teachers* (pp.163-173). Courtenay, BC: Connections Publishing and Bloomington, IN: Solution Tree Press.

Norway. 2011. Open discussion between participants at the 5th annual Assessment in Support of Learning: International Perspectives conference in Bergen, Norway, June 15, 2011.

Pink, D. 2009. *Drive: The Surprising Truth About What Motivates Us*. New York: Riverhead Books.

Reay, D. and Wiliam, D. 1999. 'I'll be a nothing': Structure, agency and the construction of identity through assessment. *British Educational Research Journal* 25, no. 3: 343-354.

Roderick M. and Engel, M. 2001. The grasshopper and the ant: Motivational response of low achieving pupils to high stakes testing. *Educational Evaluation and Policy Analysis* 23, no. 3: 197-228.

Rodriguez, M. C. 2004. The role of classroom assessment in student performance on TIMSS. *Applied Measurement in Education* 17, no. 1: 1-24.

Stiggins, R. 2002. Assessment crisis: The absence of assessment *for* learning. *Phi Delta Kappan* 83, no. 10: 758-765.

Stiggins, R. 2013. Foreword. In A. Davies, S. Herbst, and K. Busick (Eds.), *Quality Assessment in High Schools: Accounts From Teachers.* Courtenay, BC: Connections Publishing and Bloomington, IN: Solution Tree Press.

Sueoka, L. 2013. "A culture of learning: Building a community of shared learning through student online portfolios." In A. Davies, S. Herbst, and K. Busick (Eds.), *Quality Assessment in High Schools: Accounts From Teachers* (pp. 151-161). Courtenay, BC: Connections Publishing and Bloomington, IN: Solution Tree Press.

Tyler, R. 1949. *Basic Principles of Curriculum and Instruction.* Chicago, IL: University of Chicago Press.

Appendix A: Pushing Back – What About These Challenges?

What About F-1?

Assessment isn't about helping my students learn. It is something that comes at the end of learning.

Some teachers used to think that assessment is a test, performance task, or culminating assignment that has to be done at the end of a unit so that the class can move to the next topic and a grade can be entered into a grade book. It is considered an event or a thing.

Classroom assessment is understood better now. Now we know that assessment *for* learning occurs during the learning. We let students know what the learning target or destination is, we share with them what success and quality look like, and we provide them (or they provide themselves) with specific and descriptive feedback so that they can adjust what they are doing to get to that learning target. These strategies definitely help students learn.

Also, many teachers use effective classroom assessment strategies to support student learning, but think they are simply powerful instructional techniques. Murray Guest (2013), a high school mathematics teacher, wrote a powerful article indicating that math teachers are ahead of the curve when it comes to classroom assessment, but they just don't know it.

Assessment *of* learning – evaluation or summative assessment – occurs at the end of the learning. It is the time when we make a professional judgment. It comes at the end of the learning, when time has run out. It occurs when teachers make a decision and communicate to others the degree to which or the level at which content and the processes that compose the course have been learned.

The research of the Assessment Reform Group (2002, 2006) is clear in its findings. Involving students in their assessment makes a significant difference in the achievement levels of students.

How else might you respond to this "What About"?

What About I-1?

> *This process of determining how well students are doing may make sense at the elementary level, but we are preparing our students for university or college. This may not work in the real world.*

It is true. Some of our students do continue their education immediately after high school graduation by attending college or university. But not all our students follow this pathway, and among those who do start, many do not continue into the second, third, and fourth years. So, while it is important to help students to see themselves continuing on to post-secondary institutions, if that is their dream, high school is a time for students to practise and put patterns of behaviour in place that will be helpful later on, when they are no longer in school. Learning the skill of self-monitoring and self-regulating their way to success is extremely important. It is necessary that students understand what needs to be done, how their current work aligns with what needs to be done, and how they can close the gap between the two, especially outside the K-12 setting.

How else might you respond to this "What About"?

What About I-2?

> *At the high school level, there are high-stakes tests. So I can't afford to involve my students in this way.*

This is a good point. Many teachers feel the pressure of external and internal exams. It is an ever-present reality, not only in the high school. However, involving students in their own assessment – helping them to understand what is expected of them, helping them picture quality by sharing samples or co-constructing criteria, and helping them to self-monitor to success – actually prepares them for those exams and tests. Research shows that students who are involved in assessment *for* learning strategies do better on external tests and measures than those who are not (Rodriguez, 2004; Meisels et al., 2003). Furthermore, the research indicates that students whose teachers spend all their time "teaching to the test" score lower on those same external tests and measures (e.g., Berliner & Biddle, 1998; Darling-Hammond & Richardson, 2009). Assessment *for* student learning prepares students for whatever comes their way by helping them deeply understand the work that is expected of them.

How else might you respond to this "What About"?

What About 1-1?

> *Secondary curricula are jammed with standards and expectations. I don't have time to do all of this with my students.*

We recently heard a high school mathematics teacher say this aloud in a group of dozens of high school colleagues. A colleague turned to him and commented that he couldn't believe that the high school curriculum was more packed than that at the elementary level. He continued by stating that many kindergarten teachers deal with students who come to school not knowing even how to hold pencils or scissors; if students are lacking such basic skills as these, then there truly is a lot to cover.

Several high school teachers have noted that when they involve students in their own assessments, they save time. For example, at the beginning of a semester, a high school physics teacher co-constructed criteria with his students about what counted in a lab report, based on sample reports from previous years. He recognized that the lab reports that he received from his students after that process were what he would usually see closer to the end of the semester. He reasoned that he had just saved months of teaching time. Now he could teach concepts and curriculum standards earlier in the semester because he had "found time" that had, in the past, been spent going over and over what he expected from his students.

How else might you respond to this "What About"?

What About 1-2?

> *Tests and quizzes are the only way to make sure that our assessment is objective and fair. All this other stuff is too subjective.*

Tests and exams are only one way to see what a student knows. And not everything that is expected of students in the curriculum can be measured by a test. For example, students cannot be evaluated by a paper-and-pencil test in curriculum areas where they are expected to communicate orally.

Tests are not objective measures. They usually result in scores that represent a quantitative measuring system related to numbers, which is as close as a test comes to being objective. Think about this: Two physics teachers might be preparing a test for the same unit of study. One teacher creates a test of 12 questions that appeal to her and the other teacher builds a test of five different questions that have served him well in the past. By selecting questions that they view to be important, these two teachers have built in subjectivity.

Instead of asking ourselves whether our measures are objective, we need to be asking ourselves whether our measures are reliable and valid. Reliability refers to repeatability. Can the student show what he knows in different situations and at different times? Validity refers to the match of the evidence of learning to what is to be assessed – what is to be learned. And, to illustrate, let us go back to the example of an oral presentation. We cannot evaluate whether a student can orally communicate ideas to an audience by asking them to complete a paper-and-pencil test. From a classroom assessment perspective, this evidence of learning is not valid, given what was to be learned.

Teacher professional judgment is more reliable and valid than external tests when teachers have been involved in examining student work, co-constructing criteria, scoring the work, and checking for inter-rater reliability (ARG, 2006, Burger et al., 2009).

Inter-rater reliability is defined as the result of learning to make an informed professional judgment. Educators engage in a process of inter-rater reliability when they meet, create quality criteria, and build a scoring rubric for student work. The student work could include, for example, a performance task, a product, observations of application, or a body of evidence. Each educator examines and then scores the student work using a scoring rubric.

At this point, all the scores are examined for consistency among all the educators. The percentage to which they agree is used to determine inter-rater reliability. The higher the percentage of agreement among all the educators' rating (i.e., the more the scores are similar), the higher the inter-rater reliability will be. This process helps teachers refine and improve their professional judgment.

How else might you respond to this "What About"?

What About 1-3?

> *We need to make sure that our assessment and evaluations are fair, and that means that we need to use all the same assignments, tests, and tasks to determine a grade or mark.*

State and provincial standards, outcomes, or curriculum expectations identify targets that students need to reach, but they do not specify how students are to reach them. For example, a student may need to be able to describe a certain scientific concept. It does not state that the concept needs to be described only by the written word. Some students might be able to describe it in conversation or by using a labelled diagram. In other words, there is more than one way for students to show what they know.

To use a highly quoted phrase – fair is not always equal. Educators come to the profession and to the signing of a contract in many different ways. Some teachers come to the profession after having worked for many years in another field. Yet others come to teaching through the more direct route of university or college right after high school. And still others come back to teaching after time spent raising a family, taking a sabbatical, or traveling around the world. Few of us would say that the only teacher who deserves a contract is the one who has taken the direct route. However, this same understanding is not always extended to our students. Some would say that the way to a grade on a transcript or a report card is to be traveled in exactly the same way in order for it to be fair. We need to focus on providing all students with the opportunity to learn and to show what they have learned in a way that best connects to their own learning needs and strengths; we need to make this appropriate and sufficient, given what students need to know, do, and articulate as outlined in the curriculum standards or outcomes. We need to check if the student understands and can articulate that understanding. It is in the articulation that differing forms can be taken. It is not fair to say that a student does not understand the effect of modern war on society, for example, simply because he or she cannot write it down. It becomes equitable if that student has the opportunity to articulate that understanding in different ways, instead of only putting pen to paper.

How else might you respond to this "What About"?

What About 1-4?

> *Being involved in their own assessment makes sense when teachers are working with students who "get it." It just does not work with students who struggle.*

In this area, the research is exceedingly clear. Quality classroom assessment has the largest effect on student achievement ever documented (Black and Wiliam, 1998, 2003; Black, P. et al., 2003). This is true for all students, and it is especially true for students who struggle academically. From a practical point of view, this makes absolute sense. Students who struggle often do so because they do not intuitively know, or cannot "read between the lines" to determine what the teacher wants. In every class, there are students who seem to be able to learn without very much direction or instruction. However, it seems as though this kind of student in our schools is diminishing. More and more, our students need explicit information that describes what is expected of them. Students who struggle do not get enough to "go on" from comments like "Try harder," "You can do better," or "I will give you time to re-do this work." They need specific information to better understand what the work needs to look like, what counts as quality, and what in their work is correct and what needs to be changed. Sharing samples with students and providing them with criteria about what counts in the work or assignment is crucial. This is assessment *for* learning.

How else might you respond to this "What About"?

What About 2-1?

> *Only test scores and marks motivate students. We need to give them more of that. They need that kind of information.*

Many of us believe that the best way to motivate others and ourselves is with external rewards like test scores, grades, and marks. This thinking can be a mistake. Research and writing in the area of human motivation (Pink, 2009; Covington, 1998) reports that what motivates us is the deeply human need to direct our own lives, to learn and create new things, and to do better by our world and ourselves. Edward Deci & Richard Ryan (2002) and Wynne Harlen & Ruth Deakin Crick (2002) remind us that extrinsic rewards alone – like test scores, grades, and marks, which are all forms of evaluative feedback – undermine interest and motivation.

Students who are fed a steady diet of evaluative feedback tend to select tasks that are low in difficulty, with an eye to getting them done as quickly and as easily as possible. For students who struggle, receiving evaluative feedback alone can lead to feelings of rejection and alienation. Consistent messaging that they are not doing well enough does not give them the information that they need to change what they are doing. Many students have difficulty decoding what the evaluative feedback is saying. What have I done well? What do I need to change?

How else might you respond to this "What About"?

What About 2-2?

At the secondary level, I might see over 130 students in a semester. There is no time for me to do this.

What we know from the field of brain research is that even if we had a class with only one student, we would not be able to provide enough specific, descriptive feedback to maximize the learning. If we can't do it for one adequately, we can't do it for 131. So we need to involve the student. The student can give himself and his peers feedback. If we don't involve students, we miss valuable opportunities to provide feedback that can move the learning forward.

Some teachers do have over 130 students in their classes in one semester. Others have more than 500 in a week. This can be a challenge for some teachers, especially if each class they teach is from a different discipline or at a different level. Consider, though, the elementary teacher who might have 32 students in his class. He has to teach all 32 of those students English, mathematics, science, social studies, and health (and maybe more). Translated to a secondary school context, that would mean that that teacher could have 160 students over the semester. The demands from a curriculum perspective might not be all that different. No matter what your context is, you can find benefits in improved student learning and can maximize the use of your time. After all, this is an ideal way to have students working harder than their teachers – and the person working the hardest is learning the most. Why shouldn't it be the students?

How else might you respond to this "What About"?

What About 2-3?

It does not make sense to allow students the opportunity to re-do their work. They should only have one chance, and that is all.

Having the chance to do something again is viewed by some as shirking responsibility or reinforcing procrastination. But ask yourself this question: How many of your family, friends, and acquaintances required more than one attempt at getting their driver's license? Many people are not successful the first time, and yet the Motor Vehicle Branch allows them to come back and try again. What about if you failed a course at college or university? You were not kicked out of the entire program of study. You needed to try it again or attempt a different course. Why would we not extend the same opportunity to our secondary school-aged students?

When students remit their work a second or a third time, often after a round of specific and descriptive feedback, it is important that they indicate the way in which the work has changed. That is, as busy educators, we do not have time to review a piece of work a second time, to pore over that lab report, essay, or problem to realize only a surface, singular, or simple change has been made. Instead, students should be asked to prove to the teacher the ways in which that work is different and better aligns with the descriptions and expectations of quality. This might be accomplished by having the students either literally or virtually attach "sticky notes" to the spots where changes have been made. Or, this might mean that students indicate, in point form, what they did differently this time. Possibilities abound in order to allow this to happen. The key point is, though, that students have a shared responsibility with their teachers.

If we have given students feedback, can they consider it and produce the work, but at a higher level of achievement? Can we help students understand that we learn from our mistakes and the help that we have been given? Might we communicate to students that learning is lifelong and ongoing? These are important lessons.

How else might you respond to this "What About"?

What About 3-1?

> *What about the students who don't do anything in class throughout the term or semester and then, at the end, hand most of their work in and show up to take the final exam? They pass based on work that is all done at the last moment. It's not right.*

Some students have figured out that it is sometimes possible to pass in the last moments of the course. This can be frustrating. To change this, we need to re-examine our definition of success for the course. If we calculate a term or final mark based on only tests, quizzes, and a list of assignments, then, as we share this list with the students, they come to understand exactly what matters. It is only what is on the list. The learning outcomes and standards have been effectively been replaced. Suddenly we have students who figure out how to give us exactly what we have asked for and no more.

What if teachers defined success in such a way that students had to collect evidence throughout the semester to provide proof that they were reaching the learning goals set both for themselves and by the teacher? What if the evidence that they collect is evaluated and contributes to the end-of-term grade? What about a collection of evidence of learning – you might even choose to call it a portfolio – that at the end of the semester shows growth and development over time, in relation to important standards or outcomes? Could this comprehensive collection of evidence in relation to the standards and outcomes also be significant part of the final grade?

What about describing what an A or a 90-percent-plus student would look like in this class? Could you include habits of mind such as perseverance, flexibility of thought, and risk-taking? Could students show evidence of these habits of mind being evident day-by-day across the course and the semester? This is not only possible, but high school teachers have begun to share exactly how they do this (Davies, Herbst & Busick, 2013).

How else might you respond to this "What About"?

What About 3-2?

What do I do with students who turn in their work late, or maybe not at all?

Teachers work with students to help them understand that they are responsible and have a role for providing evidence of their learning to the teacher. That is part of the students' role. Additionally, students need to understand that there are consequences for submitting their work late. However, the natural consequence of not handing in assignments should be to hand them in. Some people may think having to actually hand the work in is not a consequence or perhaps not enough of a consequence. We would agree, but it is the first step towards addressing the problem.

If the first reaction to work not being handed in is to begin to deduct marks, then very quickly students no longer see a reason to submit the missing evidence of learning. These days, teachers are putting other things in place that serve as a consequence, including:

- setting up a student contract or referring students to additional supports
- chunking major assignments into smaller pieces that could be submitted in stages
- communicating with parents just as assignments are due

- providing an alternate assignment that, while still meeting the intended outcomes of the original assignment, better reflects the student's interests and strengths

If evidence of learning is not available to the teacher, then a teacher's ability to make a professional judgment is impaired. If there is not enough evidence of learning, then a grade cannot be assigned. Teachers working with their colleagues have developed a variety of strategies to support students as they work to ensure students provide enough evidence of learning. At the end of the term, when report card grades are required, teachers need to be very careful that they are not putting themselves at professional risk. Report cards are legal documents. They report what students have learned and achieved in relation to the learning outcomes and standards for the course. If the records kept by the teacher show little or no evidence of learning in relation to the outcomes of the course, then the student grade must reflect that unknowing. Some schools and systems use the abbreviation NE (which means Not Enough Evidence), and students have a certain length of time to submit the needed evidence or complete alternative tasks that give teachers enough evidence. If evidence is not available, then a grade is not assigned for the course – there is no credit recorded.

Sometimes it seems to be a matter of motivation. If our default stance is to deduct marks or assign a score of zero, then students might realize that there is nothing in it for them to turn in their work. This creates another set of problems that cannot be solved by penalties related to the grading system. The actual learning that has been accomplished is misrepresented by deductions. The baseline question is: Can/does the student demonstrate mastery of the learning that is expected in the standards? Using zeros or reducing the grade because of behavioural factors is, as Rick Stiggins has pointed out, attacking classroom management and motivation challenges (Stiggins, 2005).

Some schools and systems continue to engage in lengthy and thoughtful discussions about these issues. Your discussions might be focused around the use of zeros, deducting marks for late assignments, or some other kind of response to students not providing the kind of evidence of learning requested. As you come to a collegial decision about these matters, we remind you that the final-grade calculation must reflect the informed professional judgment of the teacher and accurately represent a student's actual achievement.

As these issues are discussed, it is sometimes helpful to have an example from outside the situation to help us better understand the issues in place. For example, some people say that in the real world, if things are late, there are consequences. What if a teacher does not complete the report cards by the specified date? Is she fired? No, she is not fired. Are her wages deducted? No, her wages are not deducted. What will happen? Likely, the principal will have a conversation with her to determine why the reports are not yet completed and to plan for next steps. This might mean bringing in a substitute so that the reports can be finished during the next school day, it might mean that a district consultant is brought in to provide support and guidance, or it might even mean that the principal spends the next two evenings sitting beside that teacher to ensure that they are done. The consequence for not doing report cards is doing report cards.

What supports can be identified so that the natural response to not turning work in is not to abandon it, but to get it done?

How else might you respond to this "What About"?

What About 3-3?

> *Some parents don't value educators' professional judgment. Some even challenge what we record on a report card.*

When parents question a teacher's informed professional judgment, teachers can choose to respond thoughtfully by engaging parents in conversation as they look at the relevant standards and samples. Samples have an important role to play in helping those outside the classroom understand the learning that is taking place. This is especially true for parents. Samples help us respond to the perennial parent question, "How is my child doing compared to the other students in the class?" The first thing we do is reframe the question so we can respond ethically. We say, "Your child, in relation to the standards or outcomes is . . . ," and we share samples of the current range of work and where their child's work is within that range. Samples also provide a strong visual to show parents how their child's work compares with what is expected.

Students also have a role to play. When they have been engaged as partners in this assessment process, collecting evidence and explaining why it is proof of learning, they are better able to explain to parents what the evidence means and what their next learning steps are.

How else might you respond to this "What About"?

Appendix B: Four-Quadrant Planning Questions

Preparing for Learning–Beginning with the End in Mind

1. Are all outcomes represented in the list?
2. In what ways does the list represent both process and product (do, say, know)?
3. Is each statement simple?

Collecting Evidence of Learning

1. In what ways will my evidence show whether or not students have learned what they needed to learn?
2. Is there any evidence that I am collecting for which I am not accountable?
3. Am I collecting evidence from multiple sources?
4. Am I collecting enough evidence to see patterns over time?
5. Am I collecting too much evidence? Is there something that I could stop collecting?
6. In what ways can my students be involved in collecting and organizing evidence of learning?

Describing Quality

1. Are samples available to show quality? Ways not to reach quality?
2. What are your plans to co-construct criteria?
3. Do you have a range of samples when learning is developmental?

Evaluation

1. Are report card grades given for the full range of educational standards or outcomes, not just those easiest to measure?

2. Has evidence of learning been selected because of its alignment with outcomes and standards?
3. Are the report card grades based upon a wide array of evidence from multiple sources over time so as to ensure validity and reliability?
4. Do students understand expectations and acceptable evidence?
5. Are students involved in co-constructing criteria in relation to products, processes, and collections of evidence of learning?
6. Does the summative evaluation take place after students have time and opportunity to learn?
7. Are report card grades derived from evidence present, not absent (thus devoid of practices such as assigning zeros, grading on a curve, averaging, or penalty deductions)?
8. Are report card grades for achievement of standards or learning outcomes reported separately from other nonachievement factors such as effort, attitude, attendance, and punctuality?
9. Are report card grades reflective of a student's most consistent, more recent pattern of performance in relation to course learning goals based on the relevant standards and outcomes, as well as pre-determined levels of quality?
10. Do report card grades reflect informed teacher professional judgment of the level of quality of student work in relation to the standards or outcomes?
11. Are report card grades validated by and anchored in collaborative conversation and analysis of student work against agreed-upon criteria by teachers across grade levels and subjects?
12. Are report card grades reflective of and illustrated by collections of exemplars and samples that illustrate levels of quality and achievement?

Anne Davies, Ph.D., is a researcher, writer, and educational consultant in the area of classroom assessment. She has also been a teacher, school and system leader, and has worked at the university level. Author and co-author of more than 30 books and multi-media resources, as well as numerous chapters and articles, she works nationally and internationally presenting to a wide range of audiences. Anne works with educators at all levels, using quality assessment practices in support of student and adult learning. Anne can be reached at *anne@annedavies.com*.

Sandra Herbst is a noted system leader, author, speaker, and consultant with over twenty years of experience. She has worked in both elementary and secondary schools and is a former classroom and specialty teacher, school administrator, program consultant, and assistant superintendent. Sandra has facilitated professional learning in schools, districts, and organizations across North America in the areas of leadership, instruction, assessment, and evaluation. Her school and district experiences deeply connect learners to practical and possible strategies and approaches. She is the co-author of three books on the topic of assessment. Contact her at *sandra@connect2learning.com*.

More information about Anne, Sandra, and classroom assessment resources is available at http://www.connect2learningresources.com/transformingassessment.html.

Resources from connect2learning

The following books and multimedia resources are available from connect2learning. Discounts are available on bulk orders.

Classroom Assessment Resources

Making Classroom Assessment Work – Third Edition .... ISBN 978-0-9867851-2-2
L'évaluation en cours d'apprentissage .... ISBN 978-2-7650-1800-1
Quality Assessment in High Schools: Accounts From Teachers .... ISBN 978-0-9867851-5-3
Setting and Using Criteria – Second Edition .... ISBN 978-0-9783193-9-7
Établir et utiliser des critères – Deuxième édition .... ISBN 978-0-9867851-7-7
Self-Assessment and Goal Setting – Second Edition .... ISBN 978-0-9867851-0-8
Conferencing and Reporting – Second Edition .... ISBN 978-0-9867851-1-5

Leaders' and Facilitators' Resources

Lesson Study: Powerful Assessment and Professional Practice .... ISBN 978-0-9867851-8-4
Leading the Way to Assessment *for* Learning: A Practical Guide .... ISBN 978-0-9867851-3-9
Transforming Schools and Systems Using Assessment:
  A Practical Guide .... ISBN 978-0-9867851-4-6
Protocols for Professional Learning Conversations .... ISBN 978-0-9682160-7-1
When Students Fail to Learn .... ISBN 978-0-9783193-7-3
Assessment *for* Learning K-12 (Multimedia) .... ISBN 978-0-9783193-8-0
Assessment *of* Learning: Standards-Based Grading and Reporting
  (Multimedia) .... ISBN 978-0-9736352-8-7
Facilitator's Guide to Classroom Assessment K-12 (Multimedia) .... ISBN 978-0-9736352-0-1

Peace Education

Remember Peace .... ISBN 978-0-9736352-5-6
Seasons of Peace .... ISBN 978-0-9736352-7-0

How To Order

Phone:	(800) 603-9888 (toll-free North America)	Web:	www.connect2learning.com
	(250) 703-2920		
Fax:	(250) 703-2921	Post:	connect2learning
			2449D Rosewall Crescent
			Courtenay, BC, V9N 8R9
E-mail:	books@connect2learning.com		Canada

connect2learning also sponsors events, workshops, and web conferences on assessment and other education-related topics, both for classroom teachers and school and district leaders. Please contact us for a full catalogue.